The Amazing Adventures of
MR. GRANT MONEY

STRIVE press

Dear Reader,

Thank you for embarking on this exciting journey with "The Amazing Adventures of Mr. Grant Money." I'm thrilled to share with you the valuable insights and lessons contained within these pages, lessons that have empowered countless individuals and organizations to achieve remarkable success in their grant acquisition endeavors.

Grant funding is a powerful tool, and this book is designed to be your companion as you navigate the intricate world of grant writing. Within these stories lie not just narratives but essential lessons that will guide you toward securing funding for your projects. As you read and engage with the exercises, I hope you find inspiration and actionable strategies to elevate your grant acquisition efforts to new heights.

Throughout my career, I've had the privilege of assisting many individuals starting from ground zero, witnessing their transformation into successful grant seekers. The stories and lessons in this book encapsulate some of the crucial insights that have contributed to their achievements.

However, I must take a moment to introduce you to another invaluable resource—the "Grant Writing That Gets Funded" training. This training has been a cornerstone in the success stories of numerous students and organizations. Tailored for beginners and intermediate grant professionals, it offers clear and comprehensive guidance. Participants not only absorb my exclusive Grant Writing Success Formula but also leave with a personalized 30-Day Grant Empowerment Strategy and Grant Readiness Resource.

Our training has played a pivotal role in agencies securing substantial funding, ranging from $25,000 to millions, in a remarkably short period. You can witness some of these success stories at WowTheyDidIt.com. I am confident that with our support, you could be the next success story, unlocking a bountiful windfall of grant funding for your endeavors.

Imagine the impact on your team as they gain insights, adopt best practices, and leverage industry secrets, giving your agency a competitive edge. This training could be the pivotal factor that distinguishes you from others, ensuring you secure the grants you pursue.

As Kjeld Linstead, a past participant, expressed, "Thanks again for the grants class a few months ago... Since taking your class, I have landed nearly $4 Million in state and federal grants for the City of Redlands."

For more information about the Grant Writing That Gets Funded training, please visit GrantWritingClasses.org. You can also secure your spot by calling 1-888-293-0284. This investment in your organization's financial stability is a strategic move towards a more prosperous future.

Best Regards,

Rodney
Grant Central USA

P.S. Be sure to try our free grant training at StrategicGrantWriting.com.

The Amazing Adventures of
MR. GRANT MONEY

Unlocking Powerful Secrets of Grant Acquisition: Mr. Grant Money's Journey

VOLUME FIVE

RODNEY WALKER

STRIVE press

Chief Editor: Laine Minerales
Editorial Assistant: Daniel Tuano
Production Supervisor: Joerje Galo
Electronic Composition: Jairus Agoncillo
Photographer: Studio 5404
Executive Marketing Manager: Jimmy Moore

Discover the breadth of our series, encompassing a myriad of crucial topics. Delve into the realms of grant acquisition, college scholarships, entrepreneurship, social impact, philanthropy, and beyond. Unearth a treasure trove of knowledge and empowerment within our diverse collection. Explore the wealth of insights awaiting you across these transformative series.

To inquire about utilizing The Amazing Adventures of Mr. Grant Money books in the classroom, securing licensing, and exploring special pricing for bulk orders, kindly contact us at info@grantcentralusa.com.

ISBN: 978-0-9659275-5-0

Printed in the United States

Dedication

In heartfelt gratitude and everlasting love to Madie Martin, our cherished "Big Mama." Your enduring love for my mother and my family has been a source of strength and joy in our lives. Thank you for embracing the role of godparent to my brother and me, and for the countless moments of guidance and support you've provided. Your kindness and wisdom have left an indelible mark on our journey. This book is dedicated to you, Madie, a living testament to the love and appreciation we hold for you. As we fondly remember Clifton Martin Sr., we honor the memory of his enduring spirit and the legacy of love he left behind. May these pages be a celebration of your profound influence in our lives and a reflection of the enduring bond we share.

With deep gratitude
and affection,
Rodney

PREFACE

The Adventures of Mr. Grant Money: A Journey of Transformation

In the world of grant acquisition, where dreams take flight on the wings of well-crafted proposals, where passion meets purpose, and where communities are transformed through the power of giving, I invite you to embark on a remarkable journey. These adventures are not just a recounting of tales but a testament to the evolution of a grant professional who started with the humblest of beginnings and emerged as a Master Grant Acquisition Specialist.

Over two decades in the making, these stories are a blend of my real-life experiences as a grant professional. They unfold the lessons learned, the challenges faced, and the victories achieved. From the time when I was a novice, wide-eyed and eager to write my first grant proposal, seeking a mere $25,000 for a youth development program, to the present, where I've had the privilege of assisting thousands of individuals and organizations worldwide each year, this journey is one of profound transformation.

It all began with the idea of sharing inspiring tales through a series of blog posts, offering snippets of wisdom and knowledge to those in the world of grants. Yet, as I put pen to paper, these stories took on a life of their own, weaving together to form something magical, something special. What started as a caterpillar of inspiration morphed into a butterfly waiting for you to leap onto its wings and embark on a series of captivating journeys.

This collection is intended to educate and entertain, to offer fresh ideas and insights for seasoned veterans of the grant profession, to guide and inspire newcomers, and perhaps even awaken the curiosity of a young student unaware of the incredible world of grant acquisition.

In this adventure, we'll dive into the core of grant writing, explore the depths of fundraising, and unearth the hidden treasures of effective philanthropy. We'll laugh, we'll learn, and we'll leap beyond the boundaries of the ordinary.

But at the heart of it all, this is a testament to the power of belief. For, as you'll discover, belief is the force that propels dreams into reality. As you journey through these tales, remember one word: BELIEVE!

Now, dear reader, join me as we venture forth into the world of Mr. Grant Money's adventures. Let's explore, learn, and transform together. The journey begins with a single page, and the possibilities are endless.

TABLE OF CONTENT

INTRODUCTION

Prepare to embark on an exhilarating journey into the mystical realm of grant acquisition, where secrets of extraordinary power lie waiting to be uncovered. In this fifth volume, we accompany Mr. Grant Money on a breathtaking odyssey through time and space, delving into captivating stories that will leave you inspired and craving the hidden treasures of grant success.

From Cinderella's midnight lessons to revelations from luminaries like George Washington Carver, Helen Keller, and Nikola Tesla, this volume unveils the wisdom, resilience, and timeless principles that underpin grant acquisition.

Experience the thrill of covert alliances and clandestine partnerships in the Garden of Grants, witness Mr. Grant Money's transformation from fashion to funding, and join him on epic quests in Denver, prehistoric times, and the Mile High City.

With lessons from the likes of Tesla, the art of visualization, and the unforgiving ascent to greatness, this volume promises to ignite your passion for grant acquisition and empower you with the knowledge to secure the funding you seek.

Unlock the secrets of grant success, discover the hidden pathways to abundance, and ascend to new heights with Mr. Grant Money. This is your invitation to a world where dreams become reality, and where you can master the art of acquiring the grants you need.

As you turn the pages of this volume, you will find yourself spellbound by captivating tales of triumph, innovation, and resilience.

Each story is a key to unlocking the doors of grant acquisition, and together, they form a grand tapestry of inspiration, motivation, and the knowledge you need to realize your dreams.

Join us as we explore the limitless potential of grant acquisition, and let the wisdom of Mr. Grant Money guide you on your journey towards securing the funding you deserve.

Your grant acquisition adventure awaits – turn the page and embark on this remarkable quest for success!

MIDNIGHT LESSONS

The Amazing Adventures of MR GRANT MONEY

Midnight Lessons: Mr. Grant Money's Cinderella Insights

Grant Acquisition Wisdom from a Magical Dream

In the heart of Milan, amidst the elegance of a luxurious hotel, Mr. Grant Money found himself engrossed in his daily thinking ritual. With his stylish attire perfectly complementing the exquisite courtyard, he allowed his mind to wander into the realm of possibilities that grant acquisition offered. As he delved deeper into his thoughts, the warm Italian sun, the scent of blooming flowers, and the gentle rustle of leaves conspired to lull him into a slumber.

Suddenly, he awoke in a world unlike any other—a grand ballroom filled with enchanting music, opulent chandeliers, and elegantly dressed guests twirling around in a graceful dance. Mr. Grant Money couldn't believe his eyes; he had been transported into the timeless tale of Cinderella.

Amidst the glittering crowd, he spotted Cinderella herself, dressed in a resplendent gown that shimmered like starlight. She waltzed with the dashing Prince, their laughter filling the air as they swirled around the dance floor.

But Mr. Grant Money knew the tale well; midnight would soon strike, and Cinderella would have to rush away, leaving behind only her delicate crystal slipper. The Prince was determined to find the owner of the slipper, the perfect match that would change their lives forever.

As the clock ticked mercilessly toward midnight, Mr. Grant Money watched the drama unfold. Cinderella's hurried exit, the lost slipper, and the Prince's quest to find the mysterious woman who had captured his heart.

Suddenly, Mr. Grant Money was jolted awake, back in the courtyard of the Milanese hotel. The vivid dream had given him a revelation—a series of grant acquisition lessons that he couldn't wait to jot down in his treasured Gold Mine.

Lesson 1: Timing is Everything - Just as Cinderella had to leave the ball at midnight, grant seekers must be acutely aware of deadlines and submission timelines. Missing the stroke of midnight, in this case, could mean missing out on a golden opportunity.

Lesson 2: The Perfect Fit - Cinderella's slipper was the key to her destiny. Similarly, grant seekers must ensure that their proposals are the perfect fit for the funder's priorities and requirements.

Lesson 3: Leaving a Lasting Impression - Cinderella left behind a unique and memorable item—the crystal slipper. Grant applicants should strive to create proposals that leave a lasting impression, making it easier for funders to remember and support their cause.

Lesson 4: Persistence Pays Off - The Prince's determination to find Cinderella ultimately led to their happily ever after. Grant seekers should never give up, even in the face of initial rejections, and continue searching for the right funder.

As Mr. Grant Money carefully transcribed these lessons into his Gold Mine, he couldn't help but marvel at the fantastical journey his dream had taken him on. And just like Cinderella, he knew that with the right strategy, timing, and determination, grant seekers could turn their dreams into reality and find their own "happily ever after" in the world of grant acquisition.

"In grant acquisition, remember that timing is everything; missing a deadline is like missing the stroke of midnight, and it could cost you the opportunity of a lifetime."
- Mr. Grant Money

Exercise: "Cinderella Grant Acquisition Challenge"

This exercise is inspired by Mr. Grant Money's Cinderella dream and aims to help grant seekers internalize important lessons related to grant acquisition.

Objective: Explore and reinforce key grant acquisition lessons inspired by the Cinderella story through a hands-on, interactive exercise.

Steps:

1. Introduce the Cinderella Grant Acquisition Lessons:
- Share the Cinderella story and the grant acquisition lessons derived from it. Emphasize how these lessons are applicable to the grant-seeking process.

2. Create Small Teams:
- Divide participants into small teams. Each team represents a "grant applicant" looking for the perfect "funder" or "grant opportunity."

3. Grant Application Challenge:
- Present a fictional grant application challenge to each team. This challenge could include a set of grant requirements, a mission statement, a budget, and a deadline. Each team's goal is to craft a grant proposal based on this challenge.

4. Timing is Everything (Lesson 1):
- Set a strict deadline for proposal submission. Emphasize that missing the deadline could result in disqualification.

5. The Perfect Fit (Lesson 2):
- Provide each team with information about the "funder" (their preferences, priorities, and requirements). Challenge teams to tailor their grant proposal to be the perfect fit for this specific funder.

6. Leaving a Lasting Impression (Lesson 3):
- Ask each team to incorporate a unique and memorable element into their grant proposal, just as Cinderella left her crystal slipper.

7. Persistence Pays Off (Lesson 4):
- Introduce a twist by having each team initially receive a "rejection" notice from the funder. Encourage teams to demonstrate persistence by reworking their proposal and reapplying.

8. Proposal Presentation:
- Each team presents its grant proposal to the larger group, explaining their approach, their unique element, and how they addressed the funder's requirements.

9. Funder's Choice:
- After all presentations, have participants, acting as the "funder," decide which grant proposal is the best fit and deserving of funding.

10. Reflection and Discussion:
- Facilitate a discussion to reflect on the exercise. Participants should discuss how they applied the Cinderella grant acquisition lessons in crafting their proposals and share the challenges they faced.

11. Action Plan:
- Encourage participants to create an action plan for applying the Cinderella grant acquisition lessons in their real grant-seeking endeavors.

12. Closing Thoughts:
- Conclude the exercise by emphasizing the importance of incorporating the lessons into their grant acquisition practices, just as Mr. Grant Money internalized the lessons from his magical dream.

This exercise combines storytelling, role-playing, and practical grant application challenges to reinforce the importance of timing, alignment with funders, memorable proposals, and persistence in grant acquisition. It allows participants to practice and internalize these lessons in a fun and interactive way, enhancing their grant-seeking skills.

"Much like Cinderella's slipper was the key to her destiny, ensure your grant proposal is the perfect fit for the funder's priorities, and you might just find your 'happily ever after' in funding success."
- Mr. Grant Money

Discussion Questions

1. In the Cinderella story, timing is a crucial element, as Cinderella had to leave the ball by midnight. How does the importance of timing relate to grant acquisition? Can you share a specific example where understanding and meeting grant deadlines or submission timelines played a critical role in your grant-seeking success?

2. The story emphasizes the concept of the "perfect fit" in Cinderella's tale, where the glass slipper had to perfectly match the owner's foot. How do you ensure that your grant proposals align with the priorities and requirements of potential funders? Can you share strategies or insights on tailoring grant proposals for the best chance of success?

3. Leaving a lasting impression is a lesson from the Cinderella story, as she left behind the unique crystal slipper. How do you approach creating memorable and impactful grant proposals that stand out to funders? What elements or strategies have you found effective in making your proposals memorable and compelling?

4. The story highlights the importance of persistence, with the Prince's determination to find Cinderella leading to their "happily ever after." In the world of grant acquisition, how do you maintain your persistence and motivation when faced with initial rejections or challenges? Can you share a personal experience where persistence ultimately paid off in securing funding for a project or cause?

5. Mr. Grant Money's dream provided insights into grant acquisition lessons. Have you ever had a dream or an unexpected experience that led to valuable insights or approaches in your grant-seeking efforts or philanthropic work? How did this experience influence your approach to grants and fundraising?

💡 Big Idea "The Midnight Countdown Grant Calendar"

Create a specialized grant calendar tool, named the "Midnight Countdown Grant Calendar." This interactive calendar would not only display upcoming grant deadlines but also incorporate a countdown feature, emphasizing the importance of timing in grant acquisition. Users could customize the calendar based on their specific interests and receive timely reminders as deadlines approach. The calendar could also include success stories and tips from grant recipients, providing inspiration and guidance for grant seekers. This tool would help individuals and organizations stay organized, ensuring they never miss the crucial stroke of midnight for their grant submissions.

🔍 Word Search

Step into the enchanting world of grant acquisition through the lens of Cinderella's timeless tale. Join Mr. Grant Money in his whimsical dream, where lessons of timing, fit, lasting impressions, and persistence unfold.

In this puzzle, discover the words related to the extraordinary adventures of Mr. Grant Money. Can you find all the hidden words that capture the essence of this remarkable story?

Now, here are the 15 words for the word search puzzle based on the story:

N	Y	T	I	N	U	T	R	O	P	P	O	E	T
E	P	T	I	M	I	N	G	N	R	A	U	T	S
S	A	P	E	C	I	N	D	E	R	E	L	L	A
R	E	P	P	I	L	S	S	S	E	I	M	I	S
E	P	E	T	N	A	R	G	P	Y	T	O	S	A
R	R	R	Y	G	P	N	E	N	H	Y	N	U	D
U	O	S	S	P	I	N	I	G	R	O	E	B	E
S	P	I	P	P	S	T	I	R	N	I	Y	M	A
A	O	S	I	N	S	N	S	C	Y	I	B	I	D
E	S	T	I	E	D	R	P	A	I	N	P	S	L
R	A	E	D	I	I	S	F	I	T	S	N	S	I
T	L	N	M	N	N	E	N	I	S	D	M	I	N
Y	S	C	U	R	E	B	T	N	T	I	S	O	E
L	N	E	I	M	P	R	E	S	S	I	O	N	T

TREASURE
DESTINY
FIT
SLIPPER
SUBMISSION
CINDERELLA
MIDNIGHT
DEADLINE
PERSISTENCE
MONEY
GRANT
IMPRESSION
TIMING
PROPOSAL
OPPORTUNITY

"Cinderella's story teaches us that timing, a perfect fit, leaving a lasting impression, and unwavering persistence can lead to achieving one's dreams, whether in the world of fairy tales or grant acquisition."

The Garden of Grants: Wisdom from George Washington Carver

A Botanical Encounter with Mr. Grant Money

In the midst of his globetrotting adventures, Mr. Grant Money found himself in an unexpected place—a tranquil garden bathed in golden sunlight. Rows upon rows of vibrant flowers and neatly cultivated crops stretched as far as the eye could see. Surrounded by this botanical haven, Mr. Grant Money couldn't help but feel a profound sense of serenity.

As he marveled at the beauty around him, he suddenly noticed a distinguished man in overalls, tending to the crops with a sense of purpose and unwavering dedication. This man was none other than George Washington Carver, the renowned botanist and inventor.

With an aura of quiet wisdom, Carver welcomed Mr. Grant Money and invited him to join him in the garden. They sat on a rustic bench, surrounded by the lush greenery, and began to converse.

Mr. Grant Money, still in awe of the remarkable man before him, asked Carver about his incredible accomplishments, particularly his pioneering work with peanuts. Carver's eyes sparkled with enthusiasm as he began to recount his journey.

"I have always believed that nature holds endless secrets waiting to be unlocked," Carver began. "In my research with peanuts, I discovered hundreds of uses for this humble legume—everything from peanut butter to dyes, plastics, and even fuels."

Mr. Grant Money was captivated by Carver's ingenuity and resourcefulness. He listened attentively as Carver shared stories of his experiments and inventions, many of which were far less known than peanut-based products. From sweet potato flour to soybean ink, Carver's creations were a testament to his boundless curiosity and innovative spirit.

Impressed by Carver's ability to see potential where others saw limitations, Mr. Grant Money asked, "What advice would you give to grant seekers striving to overcome obstacles and make the most of their resources?"

Carver smiled warmly and replied, "Always approach your challenges with an open mind. Seek inspiration from the world around you, and don't be afraid to experiment. Sometimes, the answers you seek are right under your nose, waiting to be discovered."

Mr. Grant Money nodded, taking in Carver's wisdom. He understood that just as Carver had transformed the humble peanut into a wealth of inventions, grant seekers could find creative solutions to their funding challenges by tapping into their resourcefulness and embracing innovation.

As their conversation continued, Carver and Mr. Grant Money found common ground in their shared passion for making a positive impact on the world. They bid each other farewell, grateful for the unexpected meeting that had enriched them both.

As Mr. Grant Money touched his scepter and returned to the bustling world of grant acquisition, he carried with him not only the memory of his encounter with George Washington Carver but also the valuable lessons of resourcefulness, innovation, and the boundless potential hidden within every challenge.

"Just as Carver discovered endless uses for the peanut by embracing curiosity and experimentation, grant seekers should harness their resourcefulness and approach obstacles with open minds, for the solutions they seek might be closer than they think."
- Mr. Grant Money

Exercise: "The George Washington Carver Innovation Challenge"

This exercise is inspired by Mr. Grant Money's encounter with George Washington Carver and aims to encourage participants to tap into their resourcefulness and embrace innovation in grant-seeking endeavors.

Objective: Explore and apply lessons from the encounter with George Washington Carver to cultivate resourcefulness and creativity in grant acquisition.

Steps:

1. Introduce the George Washington Carver Encounter:
- Share the story of Mr. Grant Money's encounter with George Washington Carver and the lessons learned during their conversation.

2. Divide Participants into Teams:
- Divide participants into small teams, ensuring diversity in their backgrounds and interests.

3. Grant Proposal Challenge:
- Present a fictional grant proposal challenge to each team. This challenge should include a mission statement, objectives, and a description of the problem the grant seeks to address.

4. Resourcefulness in Action:
- Inform participants that they have limited resources and budget to address the challenge. Encourage them to think like George Washington Carver, who maximized the potential of peanuts, to find creative, resourceful solutions within these constraints.

5. Embracing Nature and Innovation:
- Challenge each team to consider how they can draw inspiration from nature and innovative thinking, just as Carver did with plants, to develop their grant proposals.

6. Grant Proposal Presentation:
- Each team presents its grant proposal to the larger group, emphasizing the resourceful and innovative solutions they have incorporated into their plans.

7. Peer Feedback and Evaluation:
- After each presentation, allow time for peer feedback and evaluation. Participants should highlight elements of resourcefulness and innovation that impressed them in each proposal.

8. Reflecting on Lessons:
- Facilitate a discussion about how George Washington Carver's philosophy of resourcefulness and innovative thinking can be applied to real grant acquisition challenges. Encourage participants to share their insights and takeaways.

9. Action Plan:
- Encourage participants to create an action plan for applying resourcefulness and innovation in their real grant-seeking endeavors.

10. Closing Thoughts:
- Conclude the exercise by emphasizing the importance of embracing nature's lessons and thinking creatively, just as Mr. Grant Money did after his encounter with George Washington Carver. Encourage participants to apply these lessons in their grant acquisition efforts.

This exercise promotes creativity and resourcefulness by challenging participants to approach grant proposals with an open mind, like George Washington Carver approached his botanical experiments. It encourages innovative thinking and offers practical experience in applying these lessons to grant acquisition, ensuring participants are better prepared for real-world grant-seeking challenges.

"In the realm of grant acquisition, the spirit of George Washington Carver lives on a reminder that challenges are opportunities in disguise, and innovation can transform humble ideas into monumental success."
- Mr. Grant Money

Discussion Questions

1. George Washington Carver's botanical work with peanuts is well-known, but he also made numerous discoveries and inventions with other crops. How does Carver's approach to experimenting with different resources and finding creative solutions apply to grant seekers facing funding challenges in diverse fields? Can you share an example of applying such an approach in your grant acquisition efforts?

2. Carver's ability to see potential in what others considered limitations led to groundbreaking inventions. How do you cultivate a similar mindset of embracing innovative solutions and approaching challenges with an open mind in your work as a grant seeker or philanthropist? Have you encountered any instances where this approach led to remarkable outcomes in securing grants or funding for a project?

3. Mr. Grant Money was deeply impressed by Carver's resourcefulness and dedication to making a positive impact on the world. How do you align your grant-seeking efforts with your mission and passion for creating positive change? Can you share a specific project or initiative where your commitment to a cause has played a significant role in securing grant funding?

4. Carver's encounter with Mr. Grant Money occurred in a tranquil garden. How does the environment and setting play a role in sparking creativity, inspiration, and innovative thinking in your grant-seeking or philanthropic work? Do you find specific places or surroundings conducive to brainstorming and generating grant acquisition ideas?

5. Mr. Grant Money carried valuable lessons from his meeting with George Washington Carver. Have you ever had a unique encounter or experience that provided you with unexpected insights or approaches related to grant acquisition, philanthropy, or funding initiatives? What were these lessons, and how have they influenced your work in the field of grants and philanthropy?

💡 Big Idea "The Carver Challenge for Sustainable Solutions"

Launch an annual competition called the "Carver Challenge for Sustainable Solutions." This challenge would invite individuals and organizations to submit proposals for sustainable projects that address pressing global issues. Taking inspiration from Carver's diverse inventions, the challenge would encourage entrants to explore innovative uses for common resources in areas like agriculture, energy, and environmental conservation. Winners would receive not only grant funding but also mentorship from experts in the field, fostering a community of innovators dedicated to making a positive impact on the world.

🔍 Word Search

Step into the lush world of inspiration and innovation with Mr. Grant Money's unexpected meeting with the legendary botanist, George Washington Carver. Discover the wisdom they shared in this word search puzzle, featuring 15 words inspired by their conversation amidst the botanical haven.

In this puzzle, discover the words related to the extraordinary adventures of Mr. Grant Money. Can you find all the hidden words that capture the essence of this remarkable story?

Now, here are the 15 words for the word search puzzle based on the story:

O	U	R	E	S	O	U	R	C	E	F	U	L	M
I	V	Y	C	A	R	V	E	R	I	A	L	B	O
T	V	E	I	N	A	T	U	R	E	E	A	O	D
P	O	N	O	R	R	S	C	N	T	G	U	T	S
N	T	O	I	E	G	T	I	O	A	E	V	A	I
D	G	M	A	O	X	C	I	I	V	L	G	N	W
P	I	A	N	D	Y	P	A	T	O	C	R	I	T
Y	M	S	R	E	O	A	E	A	N	C	A	C	A
E	Y	R	C	D	R	Y	F	R	N	S	N	A	G
I	E	T	T	O	E	U	A	I	I	O	T	L	D
N	A	I	S	C	V	N	T	P	Y	M	D	U	O
C	R	O	P	S	E	E	I	S	R	L	E	W	M
T	N	E	V	N	I	I	R	N	L	T	S	N	G
M	A	L	E	G	A	C	Y	I	N	E	T	C	T

INSPIRATION
GRANT
WISDOM
DISCOVER
EXPERIMENT
LEGACY
NATURE
CARVER
GARDEN
INNOVATE
MONEY
RESOURCEFUL
BOTANICAL
CROPS
INVENT

"George Washington Carver's remarkable journey of innovation with peanuts reminds us that the world is brimming with untapped potential, and the solutions to our problems often lie in the unexplored territories of our own creativity."

Silent Inspiration: Grant Wisdom from Helen Keller's Garden

Tapping into the Power of Human Potential

In one of his incredible journeys across time and space, Mr. Grant Money found himself in a place of profound inspiration—an elegant garden filled with fragrant flowers and delicate sculptures. In the midst of this serene setting stood a remarkable woman, Helen Keller, who defied the odds to become an enduring symbol of resilience and determination.

As Mr. Grant Money approached, he marveled at the lush surroundings and the woman who, despite her profound disabilities, had made an indelible mark on the world. He extended a courteous greeting, and although Keller couldn't hear or see him, she recognized his presence through the gentle touch of his scepter.

In a world of darkness and silence, Helen Keller had developed a unique way of communicating. She traced elegant patterns in the palm of Mr. Grant Money's hand to convey her thoughts. With astonishing precision, she communicated her experiences, her challenges, and her unyielding belief in the power of the human spirit.

Moved by her remarkable journey, Mr. Grant Money engaged in this extraordinary tactile dialogue, his fingers interpreting the intricate dance of sensations in his palm. He asked Helen about her path to breaking free from the isolation of her disabilities and achieving her dreams.

Helen Keller responded with grace and determination, recounting how her teacher, Anne Sullivan, had unlocked the world for her. Through patience, persistence, and an unbreakable bond of trust, Anne had taught Helen to communicate, to read, and to understand the world around her.

As their conversation unfolded, Mr. Grant Money asked, "What lessons can grant seekers learn from your extraordinary life, Helen?"

With deliberate motions, Helen traced her response: "Believe in the potential of every individual. Embrace the power of education and mentorship. Never underestimate the human spirit's ability to overcome adversity."

Mr. Grant Money nodded, deeply moved by Helen Keller's unwavering determination and her profound belief in the limitless possibilities that exist within us all.

Before parting ways, they shared a moment of mutual respect and admiration. Mr. Grant Money realized that just as Helen Keller had transcended her profound limitations to become a beacon of hope, grant seekers could overcome their own challenges through tenacity, education, and a deep belief in the potential of their causes.

As Mr. Grant Money touched his scepter and returned to his modern-day grant acquisition endeavors, he carried with him the lessons of Helen Keller's indomitable spirit, knowing that her legacy would continue to inspire him and countless others in their quest to make the world a better place.

In the world of grant acquisition, Helen Keller's legacy teaches us the profound impact of mentorship and education. Every individual has untapped potential, and it's our duty to help them realize it.
- Mr. Grant Money

Exercise: "Unlocking the Potential: A Mentorship and Personal Growth Challenge"

This exercise is inspired by Helen Keller's indomitable spirit and aims to encourage participants to believe in the potential of individuals and embrace the power of mentorship and education in their personal and professional growth.

Objective: Promote the belief in human potential, foster mentorship, and inspire participants to overcome adversity through education and perseverance.

Steps:

1. Introduction to Helen Keller's Story:
- Share the story of Mr. Grant Money's encounter with Helen Keller and the lessons learned during their extraordinary tactile dialogue.

2. Discussion: The Power of Belief and Education:
- Facilitate a discussion on the significance of belief in the potential of individuals, the transformative power of education, and the impact of mentorship in overcoming adversity.

3. Mentorship Pairing:
- Divide participants into pairs or small groups, and assign each group a mentorship challenge. Each challenge should be related to a specific area of personal or professional development.

4. Mentorship Challenges:
- Provide a list of mentorship challenges for participants to choose from (e.g., public speaking, project management, leadership skills, academic subjects, etc.).

5. Mentorship Pledges:
- In their pairs or groups, participants should create a mentorship pledge that outlines their goals, commitments, and timelines for the mentorship challenge they selected.

6. Mentor-Mentee Relationship:
- Participants should designate one person as the mentor and the other as the mentee for each challenge. The mentor is responsible for guiding and coaching the mentee throughout the challenge.

7. Regular Check-Ins:
- Encourage participants to schedule regular check-in sessions with their mentor or mentee to monitor progress, provide feedback, and offer support.

8. Documentation and Reflection:
- Ask participants to maintain a journal or documentation of their mentorship journey. They should reflect on the challenges, the lessons learned, and the personal growth achieved.

9. Celebration of Achievements:
- After the mentorship challenges are completed, organize a celebration where participants can share their experiences, lessons, and personal growth with the group.

10. Sharing Helen Keller's Lessons:
- Close the exercise by inviting participants to discuss how Helen Keller's philosophy of belief, education, and mentorship relates to their mentorship challenges. Encourage them to share insights and how they have applied these lessons.

This exercise promotes the values of belief in human potential, education, and mentorship by engaging participants in real mentorship challenges related to their personal and professional growth. It encourages them to draw inspiration from Helen Keller's remarkable journey and to apply her lessons in their own lives.

> *"Helen Keller's life is a testament to the limitless potential of the human spirit. Grant seekers should remember that, just like her, they can overcome challenges through tenacity, education, and unwavering belief in their causes."*
> *- Mr. Grant Money*

Discussion Questions

1. Helen Keller's story is one of exceptional resilience and determination. How do her experiences and her belief in the power of the human spirit resonate with your own journey as a grant seeker or philanthropist? Can you share an instance where you or your organization encountered challenges but overcame them through determination and belief in your mission?

2. Helen Keller attributed much of her success to the guidance and mentorship of her teacher, Anne Sullivan. In the world of grant acquisition, how important is mentorship, guidance, or collaboration with experienced individuals or organizations? Have you benefited from such guidance in your grant-seeking efforts, and if so, how has it influenced your approach to securing grants?

3. Helen Keller's ability to communicate despite her disabilities is a testament to the power of human potential. In your grant-seeking endeavors, how do you tap into and harness the potential of individuals or communities to bring about positive change? Can you share a project or initiative where you've witnessed the transformative power of human potential?

4. Helen Keller's journey is a source of silent inspiration. Do you believe that the stories and experiences of individuals who have overcome significant challenges, like Helen Keller, have a unique role to play in inspiring and shaping the world of philanthropy and grant acquisition? How can such stories be utilized to create greater awareness and drive support for important causes?

5. In her tactile conversation with Mr. Grant Money, Helen Keller emphasized the importance of believing in the potential of every individual. How do you incorporate this belief into your grant-seeking philosophy and your approach to identifying projects or initiatives that aim to uplift and empower individuals or communities? Can you provide an example of a grant-funded program that exemplifies this belief?

💡 Big Idea " The Inclusive Grant Initiative"

Establish the "Inclusive Grant Initiative," a program dedicated to supporting projects that promote inclusivity and accessibility. Drawing inspiration from Helen Keller's journey, this initiative would prioritize funding for initiatives that focus on breaking barriers for individuals with disabilities. Grant seekers could propose projects centered around accessible education, technology, or community integration, fostering a more inclusive society. The program could also include mentorship components, connecting grant recipients with experts in accessibility and disability advocacy to ensure the long-term impact of their projects.

🔍 Word Search

Step into a world of inspiration and resilience with Mr. Grant Money's encounter with the extraordinary Helen Keller. Explore the wisdom and determination they shared in this word search puzzle, featuring 14 words inspired by their remarkable conversation in the elegant garden.

In this puzzle, discover the words related to the extraordinary adventures of Mr. Grant Money. Can you find all the hidden words that capture the essence of this remarkable story?

Now, here are the 14 words for the word search puzzle based on the story:

G	I	H	R	K	E	C	A	F	I	T	B	H	G
C	N	N	N	E	N	O	Y	C	E	E	E	Y	B
O	S	M	E	L	O	N	I	E	F	I	G	A	P
M	P	E	C	L	I	M	D	M	A	D	L	S	G
M	I	N	M	E	T	O	T	M	H	G	E	E	H
U	R	T	A	R	A	N	G	O	R	G	N	G	B
N	A	O	E	M	C	E	E	M	N	E	N	O	T
I	T	R	O	O	U	Y	M	E	D	L	H	V	E
C	I	S	U	E	D	H	L	R	H	E	E	E	C
A	O	H	U	D	E	L	A	E	O	G	L	R	N
T	N	I	H	E	A	G	Y	N	N	A	E	C	T
I	G	P	C	H	N	C	L	R	N	C	N	O	C
O	N	E	C	I	N	B	O	M	R	Y	D	M	E
N	L	N	R	A	L	L	G	R	A	N	T	E	L

COMMUNICATION
LEGACY
HUMAN
INSPIRATION
GARDEN
BELIEF
CHALLENGES
GRANT
MENTORSHIP
MONEY
EDUCATION
HELEN
OVERCOME
KELLER

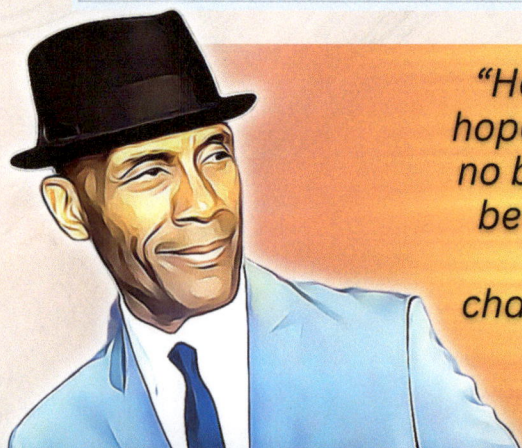

"Helen Keller's journey serves as a beacon of hope, reminding us that the human spirit knows no bounds. Through patience, persistence, and belief in the potential of every individual, we can overcome even the most profound challenges and inspire others to do the same."

WHISPERS OF IMPACT

The Amazing Adventures of
MR GRANT MONEY

Whispers of Impact: Mr. Grant Money's Covert Alliances at the Garden

The Art of Quiet Collaboration in the World of Grants

Amidst the lush and vibrant backdrop of the Huntington Garden and Botanical Museum, Mr. Grant Money arrived dressed impeccably, as always. His finely tailored burgundy velvet dinner jacket, complete with a silk cravat tie and matching pink rose corsage, drew admiring glances from fellow garden-goers. It seemed that Mr. Grant Money's sartorial elegance was an inseparable part of his persona.

As he strolled through the botanical gardens, he couldn't help but attract attention. A gentleman passing by couldn't resist giving him a nod of approval, remarking, "You're definitely the best-dressed here." Mr. Grant Money responded with a gracious smile and a tip of his hat, acknowledging the compliment in his typically charming manner.

Not far behind, two young ladies, intrigued by his attire, approached him with curiosity. One of them ventured to ask, "Why are you dressed so nice?" Mr. Grant Money, ever the diplomat, leaned in with an air of mystery and replied, "I enjoy looking nice and appreciating the finer things in life. It's my way of celebrating the beauty that surrounds us, just like these wonderful gardens."

After exchanging pleasantries, Mr. Grant Money made his way to a secluded section of the garden where his close friend, billionaire SB Steward, awaited him. Their meeting was hushed and discreet, and the specifics of their discussions remained a closely guarded secret known only to the two of them.

What the world didn't know was that Mr. Grant Money and SB Steward were plotting private ventures that aimed to add significant value to society. Their combined influence and resources were poised to make a substantial impact on philanthropy and grant acquisition, but the details remained shrouded in mystery.

The lesson from this enigmatic rendezvous was clear: **In the world of grant acquisition, sometimes the most powerful moves are made quietly and behind closed doors.** The collaboration between Mr. Grant Money and SB Steward served as a reminder that strategic partnerships and shared vision could change the landscape of philanthropy in profound and lasting ways.

As Mr. Grant Money left the Huntington Garden that day, he left behind a trail of admiration for his impeccable style and an air of intrigue about the transformative possibilities that lay ahead. His adventures, it seemed, were not only about securing grants but also about forging alliances that could change the world for the better.

Exercise: "The Power of Discreet Collaboration"

This exercise encourages individuals or organizations in the philanthropy and grant acquisition field to consider discreet collaborations, which can often lead to more profound and lasting changes in the landscape of philanthropy. By embracing partnerships that operate behind closed doors, you can leverage combined influence and resources to create transformative impacts in your community or the world at large.

1. Reflect and Identify Partnerships:
- Think about your current grant acquisition efforts or philanthropic endeavors. Are there opportunities for strategic partnerships or collaborations that you might not have considered before? Take a moment to reflect on potential allies or organizations with aligned goals.

2. Research and Reach Out :
- Just as Mr. Grant Money and SB Steward planned their discreet collaboration, research potential partners or collaborators who share your vision or mission. Look for organizations, individuals, or stakeholders that may complement your efforts.

3. Initiate Confidential Conversations:
- Reach out to your identified potential partners discreetly. Approach them with a shared vision and discuss how your collaboration could make a substantial impact on your cause. Emphasize the need for confidentiality, much like Mr. Grant Money and SB Steward's hushed meeting.

4. Develop a Shared Vision:
- Work with your potential collaborators to define a clear and shared vision for your philanthropic project or grant-seeking efforts. Make sure everyone is aligned on the goals, strategies, and expected outcomes.

5. Take Action:
- Once your collaboration is established, put your plans into motion with a focus on quiet and effective execution. Continue to meet discreetly and work together to maximize the impact of your philanthropic endeavors.

Discussion Questions

1. Mr. Grant Money's impeccable style garnered much attention at the Huntington Garden. How does personal presentation play a role in the world of philanthropy and grant acquisition, if at all?

2. What do you think Mr. Grant Money's response to the question about his attire reveals about his character and approach to life and philanthropy?

3. The story mentions Mr. Grant Money and SB Steward's secretive meeting and their plans for philanthropic ventures. How important do you think confidentiality and discretion are in the world of grant acquisition and philanthropy?

4. The story implies that strategic partnerships and shared visions can have a profound impact on philanthropy. Can you think of any real-world examples where such collaborations have made a significant difference in philanthropic endeavors?

5. How does the story of Mr. Grant Money and SB Steward highlight the interconnectedness of the worlds of fashion, philanthropy, and grant acquisition? What do you think the story is trying to convey about the power of these intersections?

Big Idea "The Transformational Alliances Fund"

Taking a cue from Mr. Grant Money and SB Steward's mission to create ventures that add value to society, individuals and organizations can establish a "Transformational Alliances Fund." This fund would pool resources from various philanthropists, allowing them to jointly invest in high-impact initiatives. By promoting collaboration and shared vision, this fund could enable philanthropists to have a more significant and lasting effect on important causes. It could serve as a model for strategic, collective philanthropy.

🔍 Word Search

Step into the stylish world of Mr. Grant Money as he explores the lush Huntington Garden and Botanical Museum, dressed to the nines. This word search puzzle is inspired by his impeccable style and intriguing rendezvous with his friend SB Steward, where they plotted ventures that would transform philanthropy.

In this puzzle, discover the words related to the extraordinary adventures of Mr. Grant Money. Can you find all the hidden words that capture the essence of this remarkable story?

Now, here are the 15 words for the word search puzzle based on the story:

A	I	M	P	A	C	T	O	I	T	L	P	R	N
L	U	E	G	E	R	R	S	T	S	E	H	L	O
E	C	E	A	D	E	P	T	S	H	E	I	B	I
B	O	G	R	A	N	E	Y	E	U	E	L	S	T
P	H	R	D	V	D	S	L	C	N	E	A	E	A
L	L	A	E	E	E	T	E	N	T	L	N	C	R
A	E	N	N	Z	R	M	A	I	E	T	R	O
C	I	T	S	T	V	A	O	I	N	G	H	E	B
I	C	L	P	U	O	T	N	L	G	A	R	T	A
N	A	E	N	R	U	E	E	L	T	N	O	S	L
A	I	N	T	E	S	G	Y	A	O	C	P	T	L
T	S	E	D	S	E	I	T	D	N	E	Y	A	O
O	O	R	R	L	S	C	O	T	I	R	G	O	C
B	O	O	O	O	N	G	D	A	A	S	H	R	O

HUNTINGTON
PHILANTHROPY
GRANT
STYLE
IMPACT
SECRETS
VENTURES
BOTANICAL
GARDEN
ELEGANCE
STRATEGIC
ALLIANCES
RENDEZVOUS
MONEY
COLLABORATION

"True partnerships and innovation happen quietly, where the world's eyes don't see, but where hearts and minds unite to make a difference."

FROM FASHION TO FUNDING

From Fashion to Funding: Mr. Grant Money's Derby Revelation

How the Kentucky Derby Inspired a Grant Acquisition Epiphany

Mr. Grant Money had traveled the world, helping countless charities and government agencies secure the funds they needed for their noble missions. But now, he was headed back to the United States for a very different adventure – the Kentucky Derby.

As always, Mr. Grant Money arrived in style. His regal velvet sandy tan dinner jacket, caramel vest, light tan cravat, cream slacks, and crisp white shirt turned heads as he stepped onto the hallowed grounds of Churchill Downs. The Derby was a spectacle of fashion and style, and though many attendees dressed to impress, none could quite match Mr. Grant Money's impeccable attire. Gorgeous ladies and fashion critics alike marveled at his sense of fashion, and he accepted their compliments with the grace and charm that were his trademarks.

Amidst the flurry of fashion and festivities, Mr. Grant Money couldn't help but turn his attention to the horses, particularly the winning jockey and the majestic thoroughbred that seemed to move with a grace only known to champions. He observed the preparation hours before the big race – the grooming, the training, the synchronized movements between horse and jockey. It was clear that these tiny details, seemingly insignificant, held the key to their incredible performance.

And then, as the Kentucky Derby unfolded before his eyes, it all clicked into place. The jockey and the horse moved as one, their synergy like a finely tuned instrument. It was a thrilling race, with horses neck-and-neck as they thundered down the final stretch. But by a mere fraction of a second, the horse Mr. Grant Money had observed so closely claimed victory.

As the crowd erupted in cheers and applause, Mr. Grant Money had his lesson: **"Winning big is often the culmination of the little things – the meticulous preparation, the tiny edges that provide an advantage. It's about paying attention to details, and understanding that even the smallest improvements can be the difference between success and coming up short."**

With this revelation fresh in his mind, Mr. Grant Money jotted down his insights in his golden journal, noting how this lesson could be applied to the world of grant acquisition. It was yet another invaluable piece of wisdom that he would carry on his journey to help others reach their funding goals. The Kentucky Derby had not only been a day of grand fashion but a day of profound lessons, and Mr. Grant Money was ever ready to share them with the world.

"A keen eye for detail can turn the tides of fortune – whether at the racetrack or in the world of grant acquisition, the small things matter."
- Mr. Grant Money

Exercise: "The Power of Attention to Detail"

Mr. Grant Money's lesson from the Kentucky Derby emphasizes the importance of meticulous preparation and attention to detail. To apply this lesson to grant acquisition or any aspect of life.

Steps:

1. Select a Goal:
- Choose a specific goal you'd like to achieve. It could be related to your work, a personal project, or a philanthropic endeavor.

2. Break It Down:
- Divide your chosen goal into smaller, more manageable tasks or components. This step is essential to understand which details require your attention.

3. Research and Learn:
- For each task, take the time to research and learn about it thoroughly. Understand what it entails, what resources are available, and any best practices.

4. Create a Checklist:
- Develop a checklist or to-do list for each task. Include all the steps or details that need to be addressed. This ensures that nothing is overlooked.

5. Plan and Organize:
- Organize your tasks in a logical sequence. Create a timeline or schedule to manage your time effectively. Plan when and how you will tackle each task.

6. Execute with Precision:
- Begin working on each task according to your plan. As you proceed, pay close attention to every detail. Avoid rushing through tasks and take the time needed to do them correctly.

7. Evaluate and Adjust:
- Regularly assess your progress and results. If you encounter challenges or find areas where improvements can be made, don't hesitate to adjust your approach.

8. Persevere:

- Maintain your focus and dedication throughout the process. Remember that it's often the smallest improvements that can make the most significant difference.

9. Reflect and Document:

- After achieving your goal, take time to reflect on the entire process. Document the lessons you've learned and the insights gained from paying attention to detail.

10. Apply the Lesson:

- As Mr. Grant Money did, consider how the power of attention to detail can be applied to other aspects of your life, including grant acquisition, philanthropy, or any endeavors you're passionate about.

"In the race for grants, just like at the Kentucky Derby, it's the meticulous preparation and the pursuit of tiny advantages that lead to triumphant success."
- Mr. Grant Money

Discussion Questions

1. How does the story of Mr. Grant Money's visit to the Kentucky Derby illustrate the importance of paying attention to details in achieving success, both in horse racing and grant acquisition?

2. In the story, Mr. Grant Money's impeccable attire is mentioned. How might one's personal presentation and style impact their ability to secure grants and build relationships in the world of philanthropy?

3. The Kentucky Derby is known for its grand fashion and style. Do you think events like this can offer unique opportunities for philanthropists and grant seekers to network and make connections? Why or why not?

4. The story emphasizes that even the smallest improvements can make a significant difference. Can you think of examples from your own experience where paying attention to minor details led to a major success or achievement?

5. How can the lesson from the Kentucky Derby about the importance of meticulous preparation and attention to details be applied to the world of grant acquisition and philanthropy? Can you think of specific areas where this lesson is particularly relevant?

💡 Big Idea "The Micro-Grants Revolution"

In line with Mr. Grant Money's philosophy of the importance of little improvements, launch a movement known as "The Micro-Grants Revolution." This initiative would encourage organizations and donors to provide smaller, more accessible grants aimed at local projects. These micro-grants would emphasize the significance of tiny improvements in various communities, focusing on initiatives that may have been overlooked due to their scale. By celebrating the power of small changes, this movement can bring about substantial positive transformations in local areas.

🔍 Word Search

Step into the world of Mr. Grant Money as he graces the Kentucky Derby with his impeccable style and keen eye for detail. In the midst of the fashion and festivity, he observes the winning jockey and horse, uncovering a lesson about the significance of small details in achieving success.

In this puzzle, discover the words related to the extraordinary adventures of Mr. Grant Money. Can you find all the hidden words that capture the essence of this remarkable story?

Now, here are the 13 words for the word search puzzle based on the story:

T	Y	G	O	E	Y	H	D	I	Y	E	T	E	O
H	N	G	Y	B	S	L	I	A	T	E	D	S	C
O	N	D	R	T	V	F	Y	N	A	N	Y	E	Y
R	S	E	Y	G	O	L	A	N	H	Y	C	L	A
O	D	U	T	G	R	A	E	S	E	K	F	Y	C
U	D	A	F	E	K	A	C	F	H	T	E	T	H
G	L	G	C	H	D	S	N	R	Y	I	Y	S	I
H	K	O	T	K	I	E	J	T	N	L	O	C	E
B	C	S	Y	V	I	C	T	O	R	Y	E	N	V
R	R	Y	G	R	E	N	Y	S	O	E	C	M	E
E	S	Y	Y	K	C	U	T	N	E	K	S	T	M
D	T	M	O	N	E	Y	E	C	T	N	S	S	E
R	G	V	U	D	S	U	C	C	E	S	S	A	N
C	Y	E	K	C	O	J	Y	D	E	V	K	C	T

FASHION
GRANT
VICTORY
SUCCESS
MONEY
SYNERGY
ACHIEVEMENT
STYLE
DERBY
THOROUGHBRED
KENTUCKY
JOCKEY
DETAILS

"Success often hinges on the ability to recognize the significance of the seemingly insignificant – a lesson taught by both champions on the track and in the world of grants."

From Struggle to Victory: Mr. Grant Money's Denver Quest

Unearthing Key Decision-Makers and Going the Extra Mile for Funding

In the picturesque city of Denver, Colorado, Mr. Grant Money had taken on a challenge that many thought insurmountable. A large nonprofit organization had been trying for years to secure a significant grant from the Department of Transportation, but their efforts had yielded nothing but poor results. Frustration was running high, and the organization was at the brink of despair.

The organization's leadership knew they needed a change, and they set their sights on Mr. Grant Money. After nearly three years of pursuing him, including a year on a waiting list with a $5,000 deposit, they finally convinced him to accept their cause.

The first step in Mr. Grant Money's plan was to conduct a comprehensive grant audit. His team meticulously reviewed past proposals, grant-seeking strategies, and the organization's overall approach. They uncovered several issues that had been holding them back: poorly defined objectives, lack of community engagement, and limited data collection on the impact of their programs. It was clear that a fundamental shift was needed.

Mr. Grant Money was unflinching in his commitment to revitalizing the organization's grant-seeking efforts. He shared his knowledge and experience, educating the team on the intricacies of grant acquisition. Together, they redefined the organization's goals, streamlined their projects, and improved their data collection and reporting processes.

But Mr. Grant Money didn't stop there. He knew that winning a $12 million federal grant required more than just a well-crafted proposal. It required building strong relationships with the key decision-makers at the Department of Transportation.

His investigative reach unearthed the names of those who held the power to make or break their grant application. Over the course of six months, he and his team developed a strategic game plan. They created a personalized approach for each key decision-maker, nurturing these relationships with dedication and finesse.

Mr. Grant Money penned letters on behalf of the organization's director, expressing the urgency and importance of the proposed project. He meticulously courted government officials, senators, and individuals of influence who could help seal the deal. He orchestrated meetings, attended conferences, and engaged in candid conversations, ensuring that the right people were not only aware of the organization's mission but were also personally invested in its success.

The day of the final grant proposal submission arrived. With a meticulously prepared grant application and an army of advocates backing the organization, Mr. Grant Money watched as the proposal was delivered to the Department of Transportation. The organization had gone beyond their comfort zone, beyond the usual, and had embraced the strategy of going the extra mile to secure the funding they needed.

And then, a few months later, the news arrived. The $12 million federal grant had been approved. The cheers of joy, relief, and triumph filled the organization's headquarters in Denver.

Mr. Grant Money smiled as he looked at his golden journal and wrote: **"Winning big isn't just about submitting proposals; it's about going over and above, nurturing relationships, and being persistent in the pursuit of funding. A grant seeker's journey is marked by brilliance, boldness, and going the extra mile to secure the resources that can create transformative change."**

As he left Denver, he knew that his mission to help charities and government agencies acquire the funding they needed continued. His next adventure awaited, and with each journey, he was not just transforming organizations but also shaping the future of countless communities worldwide.

Exercise: "Revitalize Your Grant-Seeking Efforts"

Mr. Grant Money's story highlights the importance of a comprehensive approach to grant acquisition, including conducting a grant audit, redefining goals, and building strong relationships. To apply this lesson to your own grant-seeking efforts, follow these steps:

1. Conduct a Grant Audit:
- Start by conducting a thorough audit of your organization's past grant proposals, grant-seeking strategies, and overall approach to grant acquisition. Identify any weaknesses, areas for improvement, or recurring issues that may have hindered your success.

2. Define Clear Objectives:
- Revaluate and redefine your organization's goals and objectives. Make sure they are specific, measurable, achievable, relevant, and time-bound (SMART). Clearly articulate the impact you aim to achieve with the grant funding.

3. Engage the Community:
- Enhance your community engagement efforts. Develop strategies to involve the community in your programs and projects, ensuring that their voices and needs are heard. This will strengthen your case when seeking grants.

4. Improve Data Collection and Reporting:
- Focus on enhancing your data collection and reporting processes. Implement systems to track the impact and outcomes of your programs accurately. Reliable data can help make a compelling case in grant proposals.

5. Build Relationships:
- Identify key decision-makers and stakeholders within grant-giving organizations. Develop a strategic game plan for building relationships with these individuals. Leverage both personal and professional connections to nurture these relationships.

6. Personalized Approaches:
- Tailor your approach for each key decision-maker. Understand their priorities and interests and align your proposal accordingly. Highlight how your project aligns with their vision and mission.

7. Craft Compelling Letters:
- Draft persuasive letters on behalf of your organization's director, expressing the urgency and importance of your proposed project. Emphasize the positive impact the grant would have on the community and how it aligns with your objectives.

8. Engage in Candid Conversations:

- Attend meetings, conferences, and events where you can engage in candid conversations with potential funders. Create opportunities for open dialogue about your project and how it can address their objectives.

9. Go the Extra Mile:

- As you prepare your grant proposal, incorporate the insights gained from this exercise into your strategy. Ensure your proposal reflects a holistic and well-researched approach, emphasizing the community's involvement and the benefits of your project.

10. Be Persistent:

- Recognize that the grant acquisition process may take time, and setbacks may occur. Stay persistent, and don't be discouraged by rejection. Continuously adjust and improve your strategy based on feedback and experiences.

11. Review and Adapt:

- After each grant application or interaction, review what worked and what didn't. Adapt your approach and continuously improve your grant-seeking efforts.

By following these steps and applying Mr. Grant Money's approach to your grant-seeking endeavors, you can increase your chances of securing funding and creating transformative change in your organization and community.

"In the realm of grants, success blooms when determination, tenacity, and relationships combine to unlock doors you thought were closed."
- Mr. Grant Money

Discussion Questions

1. What were the main challenges faced by the nonprofit organization in Denver when it came to securing a significant grant, and how did Mr. Grant Money address these challenges?

2. The story emphasizes that "winning big isn't just about submitting proposals." What are the key components of Mr. Grant Money's approach to grant acquisition that went beyond the proposal itself?

3. Mr. Grant Money and his team developed a strategic game plan to build relationships with key decision-makers at the Department of Transportation. How can this approach be applied to other grant-seeking efforts and philanthropic endeavors?

4. The story underscores the importance of going the extra mile to secure funding. Can you think of examples in your own experience where persistence and going above and beyond have been crucial in achieving a goal or securing resources?

5. Mr. Grant Money's mission is described as "shaping the future of countless communities worldwide." What broader impact does successful grant acquisition have on communities and society as a whole, and how can it lead to transformative change?

💡 Big Idea "The Grant Ambassadors Program"

Establish a nationwide program known as "The Grant Ambassadors Program" that focuses on building a network of individuals experienced in grant acquisition. These ambassadors would serve as mentors to nonprofits and government agencies seeking grants. By sharing their knowledge, expertise, and successful strategies, they would help organizations navigate the complexities of grant-seeking. This program could offer training, seminars, and networking events, creating a community of grant acquisition professionals dedicated to sharing their experiences and expertise.

🔍 Word Search

Join Mr. Grant Money in Denver, Colorado, as he takes on the incredible challenge of helping a struggling nonprofit secure a $12 million grant from the Department of Transportation. This word search puzzle is inspired by his journey to revitalize the organization's grant-seeking efforts.

In this puzzle, discover the words related to the extraordinary adventures of Mr. Grant Money. Can you find all the hidden words that capture the essence of this remarkable story?

Now, here are the 14 words for the word search puzzle based on the story:

N	S	L	G	E	D	E	N	V	E	R	E	T	C
O	I	N	F	L	U	E	N	C	E	E	T	R	C
I	I	P	L	H	S	U	A	L	T	L	A	A	H
T	N	C	O	L	O	R	A	D	O	A	O	N	A
A	N	R	E	I	N	E	S	Y	N	T	S	S	L
T	O	T	E	L	H	N	N	O	I	A	F	L	L
R	V	H	O	I	I	S	N	O	N	O	O	O	E
O	A	Y	R	O	T	C	I	V	P	N	I	R	N
P	T	M	O	N	E	Y	H	V	R	S	G	M	G
S	I	T	E	E	U	A	N	T	O	H	R	A	E
N	O	I	N	V	L	E	N	R	F	I	A	T	S
A	N	L	O	R	G	O	C	E	I	P	N	I	A
R	S	T	R	A	T	E	G	Y	T	S	T	O	V
T	E	C	N	E	T	S	I	S	R	E	P	N	C

MONEY
NONPROFIT
TRANSFORMATION
RELATIONSHIPS
PERSISTENCE
INNOVATION
VICTORY
CHALLENGES
INFLUENCE
GRANT
COLORADO
DENVER
TRANSPORTATION
STRATEGY

"Triumph is the offspring of resilience, and it thrives when individuals and organizations go that extra mile to secure resources for transformative change."

Gratitude Across Ages: Lessons from the Prehistoric World for Grant Acquisition

*A Journey with Mr. Grant Money into the
Time of Dinosaurs and Cavemen*

In a whirlwind of adventures, Mr. Grant Money once again embarked on a journey that defied both time and imagination. This time, his travels took him to the prehistoric era, where the world was a lush landscape teeming with life – and not all of it friendly.

As Mr. Grant Money descended upon this primordial realm, he found himself face to face with a towering dinosaur, its colossal jaws snapping hungrily in his direction. In a breathtaking display of grace under pressure, Mr. Grant Money leaped out of harm's way, narrowly avoiding becoming a prehistoric snack. The smooth maneuver had even the most ferocious of ancient predators in awe of his quick thinking.

After his close encounter with the dinosaur, Mr. Grant Money ventured further into the past and stumbled upon a group of early humans. The cavemen gawked at his peculiar attire – the snazzy bow tie, the dapper vest, and the hat that crowned his distinctive look. It was apparent that they had never seen anyone quite like him.

But despite the strange clothes and stylish accessories, Mr. Grant Money sensed a kinship with these early humans. He marveled at their profound connection with the world around them, relying on intuition and nonverbal communication to thrive in their challenging environment. In the prehistoric world, it was clear that words were not yet the primary vehicle for expression.

The first lesson of this adventure came from the cavemen's simple yet heartfelt gestures. They exuded gratitude in a way that transcended language. As he assisted them in lighting a fire to fend off the evening chill, their warmth touched his heart. In return, they handed him a heart-shaped stone, expressing their appreciation for his help and welcoming him into their fold. This was a lesson in itself – that gratitude should be not just a one-time expression but an ongoing connection between grantees and funders.

This evolved into the second lesson as he observed the cavemen's genuine appreciation. The cavemen had shown him that gratitude is a language that can create a profound connection. A mere smile, a heartfelt gesture, or a warm hug had the power to convey more than any words ever could. Mr. Grant Money realized the importance of reinforcing this connection over time and in various ways, solidifying the bond between the grantee and the funder.

The third lesson emerged as he engaged in a simple yet powerful exchange with a little caveman girl. Her heart was full of gratitude, and she demonstrated this with a heartwarming hug. In this moment, Mr. Grant Money grasped the significance of emotional connections, transcending the limitations of language and formalities. These connections were the essence of any meaningful interaction, whether it was between ancient cavemen or modern-day funders and grantees.

As he prepared to leave the prehistoric past behind, Mr. Grant Money reciprocated the cavemen's kindness by leaving a heart-shaped stone of his own as a token of his gratitude. With a twirl of his time-traveling scepter, he vanished from their world, carrying the lessons learned in the depths of history with him.

Armed with the wisdom of ancient times, Mr. Grant Money continued his remarkable adventures in the world of grant acquisition, ready to help grantees navigate the intricate realm of funding. The colorful memories of his time among the cavemen served as a reminder that the simplest gestures and the most genuine expressions of gratitude were the threads that wove the tapestry of connection, binding grantor and grantee together in the pursuit of a shared mission.

"In the language of gratitude, simple gestures become profound connections that bridge the gaps of time and words."
- Mr. Grant Money

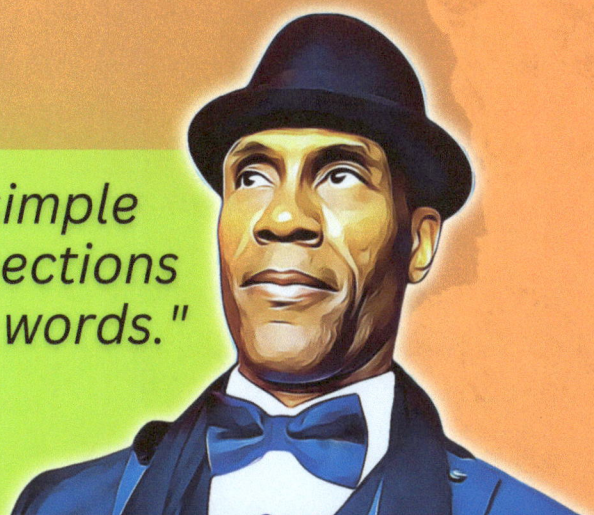

Exercise: "The Gratitude Connection"

Objective: To strengthen the connection between grantors and grantees through expressions of gratitude and genuine gestures.

Steps:

1. Create a Gratitude Exchange:
- Encourage grantors and grantees to initiate a gratitude exchange. This exchange could take the form of a simple written thank-you note, an email, a phone call, or even a video message. Both parties should express their appreciation for the support or the impact of the grant in their own words.

2. Encourage Personalized Gestures:
- Suggest that grantors and grantees go beyond the usual thank-you letters or emails. Encourage them to consider personalized gestures that are meaningful to both parties. This could be a small, symbolic gift, a piece of art, or any token that embodies the spirit of the grant and the relationship between the two.

3. Foster Ongoing Gratitude:
- Emphasize the importance of not limiting gratitude to a one-time occurrence but nurturing it over time. Grantors and grantees should find ways to continue expressing their appreciation at significant milestones, anniversaries, or moments of achievement.

4. Share Stories:
- Encourage grantors and grantees to share stories about how the grant has made a difference in their work and mission. These stories can be written or visual narratives, helping both parties understand the real-world impact of their collaboration.

5. Develop Connection Rituals:
- Suggest the creation of rituals or traditions that reinforce the connection between grantors and grantees. This could be an annual meeting, a joint project, or any shared activity that promotes collaboration and appreciation

6. Reflect on the Value:

- Periodically, grantors and grantees should reflect on the value of their relationship and express their gratitude for each other's contributions, whether they are financial or based on shared objectives.

7. Learn from the Past:

- Encourage grantors and grantees to take a page from history, just like Mr. Grant Money did during his time-traveling adventure. They should consider how past lessons, such as those learned from the cavemen, can be applied to their modern-day grantor-grantee relationships.

This exercise aims to strengthen the emotional connection and sense of partnership between grantors and grantees, recognizing that gratitude is a powerful tool for building enduring relationships and achieving shared missions.

"The power of appreciation, like a warm hug, transcends language and formalities, uniting grantors and grantees in a tapestry of shared mission and heartfelt connections."
- Mr. Grant Money

Discussion Questions

1. How did Mr. Grant Money's encounter with the cavemen in the prehistoric era emphasize the importance of nonverbal communication and gestures in building meaningful connections between individuals and organizations?

2. In the story, Mr. Grant Money learns that gratitude should be an ongoing connection between grantees and funders. How can modern grantor-grantee relationships benefit from this idea, and what are some practical ways to foster ongoing expressions of gratitude in the world of grant acquisition?

3. The story highlights that emotional connections, transcending language and formalities, are the essence of meaningful interactions. How can grantors and grantees strengthen the emotional bonds in their partnerships, and what impact might this have on the success of their collaborative efforts?

4. What parallels can be drawn between Mr. Grant Money's experiences in the prehistoric era and the challenges and opportunities faced by grantors and grantees in the present day? How can lessons from history inform and enrich modern grantor-grantee relationships?

5. Mr. Grant Money left a heart-shaped stone as a token of his gratitude to the cavemen. How can symbolism and gestures like this be incorporated into modern grantor-grantee relationships to symbolize appreciation and reinforce the sense of connection?

Big Idea "Emotional Intelligence in Grantmaking Training"

Develop a comprehensive training program for grantmakers called "Emotional Intelligence in Grantmaking." This program would emphasize the importance of recognizing and valuing emotional connections in the grant acquisition process. Through workshops, case studies, and interactive sessions, grantmakers would learn how to foster genuine connections with grantees, understand the emotional impact of their support, and navigate the delicate balance between professionalism and authentic engagement. The goal is to cultivate a grantmaking culture that values and prioritizes the emotional dimension of the funder-grantee relationship.

🔍 Word Search

Embark on a prehistoric journey with Mr. Grant Money! Join him in a world where dinosaurs roam and early humans thrive. As you search for these 15 hidden words in the puzzle, reflect on the timeless lessons of gratitude and connection. Can you find them all?

In this puzzle, discover the words related to the extraordinary adventures of Mr. Grant Money. Can you find all the hidden words that capture the essence of this remarkable story?

Now, here are the 15 words for the word search puzzle based on the story:

H	B	W	N	C	O	N	N	E	C	T	I	O	N
E	I	K	I	N	D	N	E	S	S	G	N	C	M
A	C	I	R	O	T	S	I	H	E	R	P	R	S
R	G	R	A	T	E	F	U	L	O	B	L	O	E
T	G	C	C	G	E	N	U	I	N	E	M	E
F	L	B	R	A	O	R	E	R	T	A	B	D	N
E	E	O	T	O	V	E	A	E	G	A	R	E	I
L	S	W	N	H	L	E	A	N	R	A	I	R	G
T	S	T	I	M	E	U	M	K	T	I	T	L	E
I	O	I	R	O	O	R	U	A	S	O	N	I	D
E	N	E	G	I	R	S	G	N	N	G	R	A	N
O	S	E	N	N	O	R	O	N	V	N	A	S	O
R	I	A	R	A	E	M	O	T	I	O	N	A	L
C	A	V	E	M	E	N	R	O	S	U	I	S	L

CAVEMAN
EMBARK
LESSONS
DINOSAUR
PREHISTORIC
TIME
EMOTIONAL
GRATEFUL
HEARTFELT
GENUINE
GRANTOR
CAVEMEN
KINDNESS
CONNECTION
BOWTIE

"Gratitude is the universal language of connection, a bridge that links hearts across the ages, whether in ancient caves or modern boardrooms."

WATTS OF WISDOM

The Amazing Adventures of MR GRANT MONEY

Watts of Wisdom: Tesla's Lessons for Grant Seekers

A Journey Through Time, and the Power of Imagination in Grant Acquisition

Mr. Grant Money had just finished an exhilarating grant acquisition seminar in New York City, and he was on his way to the next destination, a grand fundraising gala in honor of some influential philanthropists. The journey to the gala was a long one, and the back of his stretched limo seemed like the perfect place to catch up on some much-needed rest.

As he leaned back in the plush leather seat, the gentle swaying of the limo and the soothing hum of the engine soon had him drifting off to sleep. It was in this state of relaxation that something extraordinary happened. Mr. Grant Money found himself in an unfamiliar, yet strangely intriguing place. It was a laboratory bathed in an ethereal, blue light, and there, standing before him, was none other than the brilliant inventor, Nikola Tesla.

"Welcome, Mr. Grant Money," Tesla greeted him with a nod and a faint, enigmatic smile.

Mr. Grant Money was in awe, realizing that he had somehow slipped into a time-warp where he could converse with historical giants. He couldn't believe his good fortune and decided to strike up a conversation with Tesla, eager to learn from the genius who had revolutionized the world of electricity.

"Mr. Tesla, it's an honor to meet you," he began. "Your work on alternating current (AC) has transformed the world. But you faced immense opposition from the likes of Thomas Edison, who championed direct current (DC). How did you manage to overcome the naysayers and achieve your groundbreaking vision?"

Tesla, his eyes gleaming with wisdom, replied, "Ah, the 'War of Currents.' It was a time of fierce competition. Edison was a formidable adversary, and the world was divided over AC and DC. The key, Mr. Grant Money, was imagination. I could envision the potential and benefits of AC power, and I knew that it held the key to a brighter, more efficient future. I didn't waste my energy on disputes; I poured it into my work."

He continued, "The lesson I can impart is to have faith in your ideas and let your imagination guide you. In the face of criticism and skepticism, keep your vision clear. Edison was a great inventor in his own right, but it was the imagination and practicality of AC that ultimately prevailed."

As Tesla shared his insight, Mr. Grant Money was captivated by the elegance and resolve with which the inventor spoke. He realized the enduring relevance of these words in the world of grant acquisition. Embracing innovation, facing challenges, and harnessing the power of one's imagination were not only keys to success in the past but also invaluable principles for those navigating the intricacies of grant funding today.

Tesla left him with one of his famous quotes that resonated deeply with Mr. Grant Money: "The scientists of today think deeply instead of clearly. One must be sane to think clearly, but one can think deeply and be quite insane."

With those words echoing in his mind, Mr. Grant Money found himself back in the present, inside the limo on his way to the gala. He couldn't help but reflect on the encounter with Tesla and the timeless wisdom he had gained. In his golden journal, he wrote down the lesson he had learned: "Imagination is the key to overcoming naysayers and forging new paths, even in the face of great opposition."

> "In the journey of grant acquisition, imagination is the compass that leads us through the wilderness of skepticism towards the treasure trove of innovation."
> - Mr. Grant Money

Exercise: "Unlock Your Imagination for Grant Success"

This exercise is designed to help individuals in the field of grant acquisition unlock their imagination and harness it to overcome challenges and obstacles. Inspired by Mr. Grant Money's encounter with Nikola Tesla, it focuses on fostering creativity and determination.

1. Dream Big:
- Start by setting aside dedicated time for brainstorming. Grab a notebook or open a digital document and write down your most ambitious grant acquisition goals. Imagine the projects you'd like to fund, the lives you'd like to impact, and the changes you'd like to see in your organization. Encourage yourself to think beyond the boundaries of your current situation.

2. Identify Your 'War of Currents':
- Just as Tesla faced opposition from Thomas Edison, identify the challenges or roadblocks you've encountered or foresee in your grant acquisition efforts. Write these down as your 'Wars of Currents.' They could be issues like strong competition for limited grant funds, a lack of donor engagement, or difficulties in crafting compelling proposals.

3. Connect with a Mentor or Role Model:
- Seek out a mentor or role model in the grant acquisition field who can inspire you with their experiences and innovative approaches. Their stories and guidance can help you visualize how others have overcome similar challenges.

4. Develop a 'Vision Statement':
- Craft a clear and compelling vision statement for your grant acquisition efforts. This statement should reflect your imagination and the impact you want to create. It should be concise, inspiring, and a source of motivation when you face obstacles.

5. Imagine Creative Solutions:
- Now, it's time to channel your imagination. For each of your identified 'Wars of Currents,' brainstorm creative and innovative solutions. Consider how you might approach the situation differently, whether through new partnerships, engagement strategies, or unique proposals.

6. Think Deeply and Clearly:

- Embrace Tesla's wisdom and explore both deep and clear thinking. For each of your imaginative solutions, critically analyze the practicality and feasibility. Ensure your ideas are not just innovative but also actionable.

7. Create an Action Plan:

- Select the most promising imaginative solutions that combine innovation and practicality. Develop an action plan for each, detailing the steps you need to take to address your 'Wars of Currents' effectively.

8. Seek Feedback:

- Share your imaginative solutions and action plans with colleagues, mentors, or peers in the field. Gather feedback to refine your ideas and ensure they are well-rounded and capable of withstanding scrutiny.

9. Take Bold Action:

- With your refined and imaginative solutions, take bold action to overcome your 'Wars of Currents.' Execute your plans with determination, and don't be afraid to think beyond conventional approaches.

10. Reflect and Adapt:

- As you implement your plans, regularly reflect on your progress. Adapt your strategies as needed, remaining open to further imaginative solutions that may arise during your journey.

By working through this exercise, you can unlock your imagination and use it as a powerful tool in grant acquisition, just as Mr. Grant Money learned from his encounter with Nikola Tesla. Embracing creativity and innovation can help you overcome challenges and achieve transformative change in your grant-seeking efforts.

"Just as Tesla harnessed the power of alternating current to light up the world, grant seekers must channel their imaginative sparks to illuminate the path to success."
- Mr. Grant Money

Discussion Questions

1. How did Mr. Grant Money end up having an unexpected encounter with Nikola Tesla, and what key message did Tesla impart about achieving groundbreaking visions despite opposition?

2. The story highlights the significance of imagination in overcoming challenges and skepticism. Can you think of examples from your own experiences where imagination and innovation played a crucial role in achieving a goal or overcoming obstacles?

3. Tesla's quote, "The scientists of today think deeply instead of clearly," raises the importance of clear thinking and embracing imaginative ideas. How can this concept apply to the field of grant acquisition and philanthropy?

4. Mr. Grant Money's journey with Tesla led to a reflection on the timeless wisdom that imagination can help overcome naysayers. What practical steps can grant seekers and philanthropists take to harness the power of their imagination in their endeavors?

5. The encounter with Nikola Tesla took place within a time-warp in Mr. Grant Money's journey. If you could meet any historical figure and have a conversation with them, who would it be, and what would you hope to learn or discuss with them?

💡 **Big Idea** "Tesla Talks: Imagining the Future of Philanthropy"

Organize a series of philanthropy events or seminars called "Tesla Talks" that bring together thought leaders, philanthropists, and grant seekers to discuss the power of imagination in driving innovative and impactful grant acquisition. During these events, participants can share their stories of using imaginative strategies to secure funding and explore the practical applications of visionary thinking in philanthropy. This platform would inspire grant seekers to push boundaries, nurture creative approaches, and find imaginative solutions to secure the resources they need.

🔍 Word Search

Join Mr. Grant Money on a journey through time and imagination as he encounters the brilliant inventor, Nikola Tesla, and learns a timeless lesson about the power of vision and innovation. This word search puzzle is inspired by his extraordinary experience.

In this puzzle, discover the words related to the extraordinary adventures of Mr. Grant Money. Can you find all the hidden words that capture the essence of this remarkable story?

Now, here are the 15 words for the word search puzzle based on the story:

```
P G I E I N N O V A T I O N
T S R A L O K I N I A A D Y
I O A A L I N V E N T O R I
M N E N N I N A A E S W T M
E K L I E T I E S M R C R A
W O E O P P O S I T I O N G
A R C O I W M A V T I A L I
R A T I A I P O V R C I N N
P E R E R S T N N I E I I A
U L I E T D G K N E S M T T
N C C T I O A N T I Y I M I
I P I G I M A P T S D S O O
T T T C T E S L A O I R A N
E T Y E N C O U N T E R L T
```

GRANT
OPPOSITION
WISDOM
INNOVATION
MONEY
ENCOUNTER
VISION
TIME-WARP
TESLA
INVENTOR
NIKOLA
CLEAR
ELECTRICITY
IMAGINATION
SANE

"Imagination is the bridge between what is perceived as impossible and what is attainable; it's the catalyst for groundbreaking change."

VISUALIZING SUCCESS

Visualizing Success: The Ancient Art of Grant Acquisition

Exploring Egypt's Hieroglyphics and Unleashing the Power of Visual Storytelling

In the land of ancient mysteries and timeless wonders, Mr. Grant Money found himself in Egypt, embarking on an extraordinary expedition. As he journeyed through this captivating country, he was immediately struck by the power of storytelling through hieroglyphics and visuals that adorned the walls of temples and tombs.

Amongst the grandeur of the pyramids and the enigmatic smile of the Sphinx, Mr. Grant Money realized that, just as in the world of ancient Egyptians, visual storytelling was a vital tool in grant acquisition. These intricate drawings and symbols conveyed stories, ideas, and knowledge across generations, much like the mission of nonprofits and government agencies seeking funding.

He wandered through temples, captivated by the vivid scenes that depicted the daily life of the pharaohs, the rituals of the ancient gods, and the victories in great battles. It became clear to him that the power of visuals was timeless; it bridged the gap between the past and the present, much like the connection grant professionals must establish between donors and their causes.

Mr. Grant Money gathered insights from this ancient wisdom. He believed that, just as hieroglyphics conveyed complex ideas in a compelling manner, grant proposals should employ visuals to tell a compelling story. These visuals could be graphs, images, or infographics, all designed to help funders connect on a deeper level with the organization's mission and vision.

As he sat in the shadow of the Sphinx, Mr. Grant Money contemplated the significance of these insights. He knew that grant professionals could transform their proposals by leveraging the power of visuals. When they wove a compelling narrative with the aid of impactful images, it could greatly enhance their ability to secure funding.

With a profound quote etched in his golden journal, Mr. Grant Money summed up the lesson: "Visuals are the hieroglyphics of the modern grant proposal, bridging the gap between organizations and their funders."

As he left the land of the pyramids and hieroglyphics behind, Mr. Grant Money knew that he had unearthed a powerful lesson. He was determined to share this insight with grant professionals worldwide, encouraging them to harness the might of visual storytelling in their grant appeals. With this newfound wisdom, he was ready to continue his journey, helping organizations secure the funding they needed to make a lasting impact on the world.

> "Just as hieroglyphics conveyed the essence of ancient stories, visuals in grant proposals illuminate the purpose and impact of organizations, bridging the gap between donors and their causes."
> - Mr. Grant Money

Exercise: "Visual Storytelling for Effective Grant Proposals"

Visual storytelling is a powerful tool in grant acquisition, allowing organizations to convey their mission and vision in a compelling manner. To implement this concept in your grant proposals, follow this actionable exercise:

Step:

1. Understand Your Narrative:
- Take time to clearly define your organization's mission, vision, and the impact you aim to create. Ensure that everyone in your team has a deep understanding of your narrative.

2. Identify Key Messages:
- List the key messages you want to convey to potential funders. What are the most important aspects of your organization's work that you want them to know?

3. Create Visual Elements:
- Develop visual elements that complement your narrative. This can include graphs, charts, images, infographics, and even short videos. Choose visuals that best represent your key messages.

4. Ensure Consistency:
- Make sure your visual elements align with your organization's branding, mission, and the specific grant proposal you're working on.

5. Integrate Visuals:
- Incorporate these visual elements strategically within your grant proposal. Use them to enhance your narrative, clarify data, and emphasize critical points. Visuals should seamlessly support your text.

6. Solicit Feedback:
- Share your grant proposal, including the visual elements, with colleagues or peers, and gather their feedback. Ensure that your visuals effectively complement your narrative and that your message remains clear.

7. Review and Revise:
- Based on the feedback received, revise your grant proposal as necessary. Fine-tune the visuals to ensure they align with the narrative and are engaging.

8. Test with a Small Audience:
- Before submitting your grant proposal, test it with a small, diverse audience to gauge their reactions. Use their feedback to make further improvements.

9. Finalize and Submit:
- Make your final revisions, and when satisfied that your visuals effectively tell your organization's story, submit your grant proposal to potential funders.

10. Evaluate the Impact:
- After receiving responses to your grant proposal, assess the impact of visual storytelling on your success rate. Track how funders respond to the enhanced narrative with visuals and adjust your future grant proposals accordingly.

By implementing this exercise, you'll harness the power of visual storytelling to create grant proposals that not only convey your mission effectively but also leave a lasting impression on your potential funders.

"In the world of grant acquisition, pictures speak a language that transcends time, connecting the aspirations of ancient Egyptians to the missions of modern nonprofits."
- Mr. Grant Money

Discussion Questions

1. How does Mr. Grant Money's experience in Egypt, where he discovered the power of hieroglyphics and visual storytelling, relate to the field of grant acquisition and nonprofit funding efforts?

2. What are some specific examples of how ancient Egyptian visual storytelling techniques, such as hieroglyphics, can be applied to modern grant proposals and nonprofit communications to enhance their effectiveness?

3. In what ways can visuals like graphs, images, and infographics help bridge the gap between nonprofit organizations and their potential funders, as highlighted in Mr. Grant Money's journey through Egypt?

4. Mr. Grant Money's quote, "Visuals are the hieroglyphics of the modern grant proposal," emphasizes the importance of visual storytelling. How can grant professionals leverage this concept to create more compelling and successful grant proposals?

5. How can nonprofit organizations and government agencies implement the lessons from Mr. Grant Money's experience in Egypt to improve their grant acquisition strategies and enhance their ability to secure funding for their missions?

Big Idea "Interactive Visual Grant Proposals"

Create grant proposals that incorporate interactive visuals, such as digital storytelling platforms or virtual reality experiences. This would allow grant seekers to immerse funders in their organization's mission and impact, making the process more engaging and memorable.

🔍 Word Search

Embark on an ancient and inspiring word search journey inspired by the adventures of Mr. Grant Money in the land of Egypt. As he explored this captivating country and marveled at the power of visual storytelling, he uncovered valuable lessons for grant acquisition.

In this puzzle, discover the words related to the extraordinary adventures of Mr. Grant Money. Can you find all the hidden words that capture the essence of this remarkable story?

Now, here are the 15 words for the word search puzzle based on the story:

Y	S	I	T	S	S	I	P	T	W	I	I	Y	W
C	C	E	P	X	G	I	Y	X	O	N	S	O	G
O	I	G	Y	G	R	A	N	T	S	S	S	H	S
N	H	P	G	L	D	R	Y	S	N	I	T	I	S
N	P	S	E	I	I	H	N	S	N	G	O	F	N
E	Y	I	S	L	A	U	S	I	V	H	R	U	A
C	L	M	O	E	I	R	V	E	H	T	Y	N	R
T	G	A	P	Y	R	A	M	I	D	S	T	D	R
I	O	G	T	S	R	S	I	R	O	I	E	E	A
O	R	E	C	X	N	I	H	P	S	I	L	R	T
N	E	S	F	M	O	N	E	Y	I	H	L	S	I
W	I	S	D	O	M	E	P	I	H	X	I	S	V
Y	H	D	S	G	O	Y	O	I	G	S	N	A	E
I	P	R	O	P	O	S	A	L	S	M	G	L	R

PYRAMIDS
NARRATIVE
IMAGES
GRANT
VISUALS
PROPOSALS
FUNDERS
STORYTELLING
EGYPT
HIEROGLYPHICS
SPHINX
INSIGHTS
WISDOM
MONEY
CONNECTION

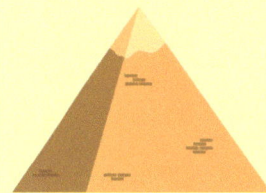

"Visual storytelling is a universal language that can unlock the doors to funding, allowing organizations to leave an indelible mark on the world through their compelling narratives."

SCALING NEW HEIGHTS

The Amazing Adventures of

MRGRANTMONEY

Scaling New Heights: The Unforgiving Ascent of Mr. Grant Money

Conquering Everest and Lessons for Grant Acquisition in the Himalayas

High above the world, in the unforgiving realm of the Himalayas, stood the formidable Mount Everest. Mr. Grant Money, who had traveled across the globe on countless adventures, found himself in an environment he had never imagined. He was about to embark on a journey to climb the world's tallest peak, and this was a mission he hadn't taken lightly.

Joining him were a team of daring climbers, each with their aspirations and dreams of conquering Everest. Their faces were weather-beaten, and their breaths visible in the freezing air, as they gathered at base camp, preparing for the daunting ascent.

As they began their climb, Mr. Grant Money couldn't help but reflect on his many experiences in the world of grants. He'd spent countless hours in chilly conference rooms, but the idea of climbing mountains was a whole new world for him. Yet, he was determined to embrace this challenge, not just for the sake of personal conquest but to glean insights that could benefit his mission to help charities and government agencies acquire vital funding.

The journey was relentless, with fierce winds, treacherous terrain, and unpredictable weather. The climbers battled exhaustion, and as they ascended, some of them had to bow out, realizing that the relentless mountain was more than they could endure.

But Mr. Grant Money pressed on, his resolve unwavering. With each step, he contemplated the words of "perseverance." Its etymology, "per" meaning "through" and "severe" meaning "that which is harsh or trying," echoed in his mind. He realized that this journey was indeed an embodiment of the word itself, enduring through the severe.

With each arduous step, he was reminded of the challenges faced by grant professionals. The relentless hours, the painstaking research, and the unwavering pursuit of funding for vital causes. Perseverance, he concluded, was an essential quality in the world of grant acquisition.

Reaching the summit of Mount Everest was an incredible feat, but Mr. Grant Money's greatest takeaway from this extraordinary adventure was the lesson of patience, perseverance, and persistence. The etymology of these words rang true in his heart. Through severe challenges, they endured. And in the realm of grant acquisition, these qualities were equally essential.

As he later recorded in his golden journal, Mr. Grant Money knew that it wasn't just about reaching the summit, but about the unwavering determination to overcome adversity. He was inspired to bring this lesson back to his work, reminding grant professionals that, like climbing a mountain, their journey to secure funding could be steep, but with patience, perseverance, and persistence, they could conquer any challenge that came their way.

With this newfound wisdom etched in his heart, Mr. Grant Money descended from the majestic heights of Everest, ready to continue his incredible adventures and bring valuable insights to the world of grant acquisition.

"Just as the relentless mountain tests climbers' perseverance, grant acquisition challenges test professionals' resilience. The unwavering pursuit of funding, through the harshest of trials, defines our mission."
- Mr. Grant Money

Exercise: "The Perseverance Journal"

Objective: To develop and strengthen the quality of perseverance by maintaining a journal and reflecting on your journey through challenges and setbacks, just like Mr. Grant Money's ascent of Mount Everest.

Instructions:

1. Get a Journal:
- Start by acquiring a dedicated journal or notebook where you'll document your experiences, challenges, and moments that test your perseverance.

2. Set a Goal:
- Choose a specific goal or challenge you want to work on. It can be related to your professional life, personal development, a hobby, or any aspect of your life where you want to build perseverance.

3. Daily Entries:
- Every day, set aside some time for journaling. Write about the obstacles, difficulties, and setbacks you encountered in pursuit of your chosen goal or challenge.

4. Reflect:
- For each challenge you face, reflect on how it tested your patience and perseverance. Describe the emotions, thoughts, and actions you took to overcome or navigate through the difficulties.

5. Progress and Growth:
- Document your progress, no matter how small, and how you learned from your experiences. Celebrate your achievements and identify areas where you could improve.

6. Encourage Yourself:
- Write motivating and positive affirmations that encourage you to keep going. Use Mr. Grant Money's lesson of perseverance in the face of adversity as inspiration.

7. Regularly Review:
- Periodically review your journal to observe patterns, track your growth, and understand how your perseverance is evolving over time.

8. Share and Connect:
- Consider sharing your journal entries with a trusted friend, mentor, or colleague. Sharing your experiences and insights can provide valuable feedback and encouragement.

9. Adjust and Adapt:
- As you continue to work on your goal, make adjustments to your approach based on the lessons and insights gained through your perseverance journal.

10. Continue and Grow:
- Maintain your perseverance journal as an ongoing practice. The act of consistently recording your experiences and demonstrating resilience will help you develop and enhance this important quality.

By maintaining "The Perseverance Journal," you'll not only develop a deeper understanding of your ability to endure challenges but also gain insights that can be applied to your professional endeavors, just as Mr. Grant Money did in his quest to secure funding for noble causes.

> *"In the heart of adversity, on the summit of Everest or in the grant acquisition arena, it's not just about reaching the peak; it's about having the heart to endure through the severe."*
> *-Mr. Grant Money*

Discussion Questions

1. What motivated Mr. Grant Money to embark on the challenging journey to climb Mount Everest, and how did he draw parallels between this adventure and his work in the world of grant acquisition?

2. In what ways did Mr. Grant Money's experience on Mount Everest reinforce the significance of perseverance and resilience, not only for climbers but also for professionals in the grant acquisition field?

3. How did Mr. Grant Money's understanding of the etymology of the word "perseverance" (i.e., "per" meaning "through" and "severe" meaning "that which is harsh or trying") influence his perspective on facing challenges in both mountain climbing and grant acquisition?

4. Can you think of other professions or fields where the qualities of patience, perseverance, and persistence are as essential as they are in grant acquisition and mountain climbing? How do these qualities apply in those contexts?

5. Mr. Grant Money's greatest takeaway from his Everest climb was the importance of patience, perseverance, and persistence. How can professionals in grant acquisition actively cultivate and apply these qualities in their work to overcome obstacles and secure funding for their causes?

💡 **Big Idea** "Grant Acquisition Resilience Toolkit"

Create a comprehensive toolkit for grant acquisition professionals, designed to help them navigate the difficulties of securing funding. This toolkit could include resources, strategies, and inspirational content that promotes perseverance, patience, and persistence. It might also feature case studies of successful grant acquisition efforts that highlight the importance of enduring through challenges.

🔍 Word Search

Welcome to the "Mr. Grant Money Wordsearch Puzzle." In this word search, you will embark on an adventure much like that of Mr. Grant Money, who ventured to the unforgiving Himalayas and conquered Mount Everest. As you navigate through this puzzle, you'll explore the theme of perseverance, which is the key to achieving success, whether it's scaling mountains or securing vital funding.

In this puzzle, discover the words related to the extraordinary adventures of Mr. Grant Money. Can you find all the hidden words that capture the essence of this remarkable story?

Now, here are the 15 words for the word search puzzle based on the story:

T	N	E	T	I	E	N	P	P	T	I	M	H	T
R	O	E	C	A	A	P	A	E	E	O	L	E	S
N	I	S	N	R	E	E	T	R	I	R	S	L	E
O	T	U	E	E	T	E	I	S	R	E	T	N	C
I	A	M	T	E	U	O	E	E	E	S	R	T	L
T	N	M	E	G	A	E	N	V	H	O	C	A	I
I	I	I	R	N	X	V	C	E	T	L	O	S	M
D	M	T	R	I	C	E	E	R	A	V	N	C	B
E	R	L	A	D	N	R	R	A	E	E	Q	E	E
P	E	A	I	N	H	E	N	N	W	E	U	N	R
X	T	T	N	U	V	S	E	C	N	I	E	T	S
E	E	I	E	F	N	T	R	E	C	N	S	N	R
A	D	V	E	V	T	E	E	G	E	D	T	X	W
U	N	L	E	E	C	H	A	L	L	E	N	G	E

VITAL
WEATHER
PERSEVERANCE
EVEREST
CONQUEST
ASCENT
DETERMINATION
EXPEDITION
RESOLVE
CHALLENGE
SUMMIT
TERRAIN
FUNDING
PATIENCE
CLIMBERS

"Perseverance is the driving force behind conquering the highest peaks and securing the most ambitious goals. Whether climbing mountains or navigating the world of grants, enduring through adversity is the true measure of success."

AFTERWARD

As you conclude your exploration of The Amazing Adventures of Mr. Grant Money, Volume 5, I trust you've found inspiration in the thrilling narratives that have unfolded. Through Mr. Grant Money's exploits, we've delved into the intricate world of grants and philanthropy, discovering both the challenges and triumphs that define this landscape.

Beyond the enthralling tales lies a reservoir of knowledge, each story a beacon illuminating the path to successful grant acquisition. Yet, the true alchemy transpires when you translate these lessons into action. Knowledge, after all, is not merely a collection of words on a page; it's a catalyst for transformation. It's the key that opens the door to boundless opportunities, but it's up to you to step through.

In the realm of grant acquisition, we all commence at ground zero. The divide between those who attain greatness and the rest lies in the resolve to transcend that starting point. As you absorb the wisdom embedded in these stories, take a moment to contemplate how these lessons can breathe life into your own journey in grant acquisition.

But the adventure doesn't conclude here! If you've relished Mr. Grant Money's escapades, consider revisiting Volumes 1 through 4. Alternatively, explore our Grant Acquisition Affirmations and delve into the nuances of Grant Writing Terminology. These resources are stepping stones to further enrichment, guiding you toward a deeper understanding of the grant acquisition realm.

Remember, this journey is a continuum. The pages may end, but your story does not. The pursuit of knowledge is akin to an ever-expanding treasure trove—limitless and ever-growing. Embrace the perpetual cycle of learning and adaptation. Much like Mr. Grant Money, you too can realize remarkable outcomes in the realm of grants and philanthropy.

For those seeking additional guidance and tools, consider navigating to GrantCentralUSA.com and GrantAcquisition.com. These platforms are treasure troves in themselves, offering an array of resources, courses, and expert insights to hone your grant acquisition skills.

As you traverse this path, understand that success in grant acquisition is not just about acquiring knowledge; it's about applying it. Mr. Grant Money's adventures illustrate that each escapade is an opportunity for growth, and your journey mirrors this truth. The power to effect change in your community and beyond is within reach.

Prepare yourself for the forthcoming volumes of Mr. Grant Money's incredible adventures, and persist in transforming your grant acquisition endeavors into tales of triumph. Your journey is only in its infancy, and the horizon is boundless. The world of grants and philanthropy eagerly anticipates your story, and the possibilities are infinite. The baton is now in your hands—run with it, and let your narrative unfold.

ABOUT THE AUTHOR

Rodney Walker is a man on a mission. He's dedicated his life to helping others secure funding for their projects and dreams. As the President of Grant Central USA, a grant development training firm internationally known for helping organizations land six-figure and seven-figure grants and shave months off the time it takes to get funded, Rodney has helped clients raise over half a billion dollars in grants!

He's also an author of numerous books, online courses and the founder of two popular grant writing conferences: The Education Grants Conference and First Responders Grants Conference. Grant Central USA has also partnered with several universities, including Regis University, Hawaii University, Oklahoma University, National University, Cal Poly University, and Florida Atlantic University.

Rodney is even the host of four podcasts: Get Funded with Rodney, Grant Writing Today, Grant Business Show, and Schools Winning Grants. He oversees Grant Success Advisors, an elite network of approved licensees who deliver today's leading training in grant development systems.

He has an extensive network of high-level contacts, including his Grant Writers Association group on Linkedin with over 15,000+ members.

Considered a national authority in the grant industry, Grant Central USA's clients have included, The Magic Johnson Foundation, the George W. Bush Foundation, Ben Guillory and Danny Glover of the Robey Theatre Company, Hawaii State Teachers Association, United Way, Habitat for Humanity, and numerous school districts and city governments.

Rodney has produced over 730 videos on grant development on his popular YouTube channel and has taught over 240,000 people how to improve their grant writing efforts. "We have been helping our clients successfully get funded and launch new careers in grant writing since 2006 across the U.S. and worldwide, giving them both the competence and the confidence to win the grants at a high level."

He says his primary specialty is "Getting our clients funded with six-figure and seven-figure grants while helping grant professionals get paid what they are worth!"

In addition to his leadership experience at Grant Central USA, he has years of experience in Business and Professional Development in various sectors. He has been a sought-after expert in grant professional development, coaching, and the law of success.

As a media personality, he has interviewed numerous celebrities, including Snoop Dogg, Heisman Trophy Winners: Reggie Bush, Charles Woodson, Professional Boxer Laila Ali, America's Next Top Model Season 19 Winner: Laura James, NBA Champions: Draymond Green, Matt Barnes, National College Football Champions: Coach Mack Brown, and Vince Young, and countless others.

It's safe to say that Rodney knows his stuff regarding grants and working with champions!

GRANT MONEY MAGNET™

I am the Grant Money Magnet™, a relentless force that navigates the intricate maze of grant acquisition with unwavering determination and a strategic mind. Challenges are not obstacles; they are opportunities waiting to be seized. With every hurdle, I rise, armed with innovative solutions, pushing the boundaries of what's possible. My curiosity is my compass, guiding me through the maze of grant landscapes, uncovering hidden opportunities and transforming challenges into triumphs.

In the realm of grant development campaigns, I am the orchestrator of a symphony that goes beyond the basics of mere grant writing. My daily actions are a testament to my commitment, with well-defined grant goals propelling me forward. I am not a lone warrior; I am part of a powerful grant team, where collaboration amplifies our impact. Together, we transcend the ordinary, transforming aspirations into tangible results.

Grant funding doesn't elude me; I attract it with an irresistible magnetic force. My mind is a powerhouse of ideas, a generator of solutions that resonate with the aspirations of benefactors and the needs of society. Relentlessness is my mantra; there's no door I can't open, no avenue left unexplored. I don't just pursue grants; I nurture relationships, cultivating a network of allies who share my passion for impact. In my grant pursuit, I don't just raise funds; I raise friends and partners, forging alliances that extend beyond transactions into enduring collaborations.

As the architect of my grant destiny, I recognize that true power lies not just in acquiring funds but in the collective strength of a united effort. I am not merely a seeker of grants; I am a catalyst for transformative change. With each campaign, I etch my mark on the maze of philanthropy, weaving a narrative of impact that transcends the ordinary. Together with my grant team, I shape a future where challenges bow before innovation, and the resonance of our collaborative endeavors echoes through the corridors of progress. Grant by grant, we sculpt a legacy that stands as a testament to the limitless potential of unified action and unwavering dedication.

Recite and embrace the power of this statement daily; let its resonance shape your mindset and fuel your unwavering commitment to grant success.

GRANTOPOLY ROYAL RULES

Dive into a realm of funding mastery with Mr. Grant Money's 10 Grantopoly Royal Rules For Engagement - your strategic guide to securing maximum funding for your organization. Revisit these rules often and witness your grant success soar as you put them into practice! 🚀 💲 #GrantMastery #FundingSuccess

1. 🎯 **Master the Mission:** Clearly articulate your organization's mission in every proposal, demonstrating an unwavering commitment to your cause.

2. 🌟 **Impact is King:** Highlight the tangible, life-changing impact of your projects; grantors want to see real results.

3. 🤝 **Build Strategic Alliances:** Showcase partnerships with other organizations to demonstrate a united front in achieving common goals.

4. 📊 **Data Speaks Louder:** Back your proposals with compelling data and statistics that underscore the urgency and necessity of your work.

5. 📖 **Storytelling Magic:** Craft narratives that evoke empathy, connecting the funder emotionally to your mission and beneficiaries.

6. 💲 **Budget Brilliance:** Develop meticulously detailed budgets that align with project goals and ensure every dollar is well-spent.

7. 📈 **Transparent Metrics:** Articulate clear and measurable outcomes, outlining how the funding will drive positive change.

8. 🌐 **Engage the Community:** Illustrate strong community involvement and support, reflecting a broad network invested in your success.

9. 🔄 **Continuous Learning:** Demonstrate a commitment to improvement through feedback loops and adaptive strategies.

10. 🙏 **Express Gratitude:** Always express sincere gratitude for the grantor's consideration, building a foundation for long-term partnerships.

MR. GRANT MONEY'S IDIOMS

Welcome to a world of financial creativity and linguistic flair! In this collection, you'll find ten unique "Mr. Grant Money" idioms crafted to add a touch of wit and imagination to your discussions about grants and funding opportunities. These idioms are not just expressions; they're windows into the dynamic and often challenging realm of grant acquisition. Enjoy more of these with new ones in the next volumes.

1. **Granting the Wisdom of the Elders:**
Meaning: Drawing upon the knowledge and experience of seasoned professionals in the field of grant acquisition.

2. **Dancing on the Edge of Grant Precipice:**
Meaning: Taking calculated risks in pursuing ambitious and innovative grant projects.

3. **Granting the Quantum Leap:**
Meaning: Making significant advancements or breakthroughs with the support of transformative grant funding.

4. **Painting with the Colors of Grant Diversity:**
Meaning: Embracing a wide range of grant opportunities and sources to enhance overall funding diversity.

5. **The Grant Nomad's Journey:**
Meaning: Traveling across various sectors and regions in search of diverse grant opportunities.

6. **Granting the Beacon of Progress:**
Meaning: Signifying positive change and advancement achieved through successful grant projects.

7. **Plucking Grant Stars from the Sky:**
Meaning: Successfully securing elusive or highly competitive grant opportunities.

8. **Dusting off the Grant Crystal Ball:**
Meaning: Attempting to predict future trends and opportunities in the ever-evolving grant landscape.

9. **Granting the Velvet Glove Approach:**
Meaning: Handling grant applications and interactions with a smooth and diplomatic touch.

10. **The Grant Symphony Reprise:**
Meaning: Building upon previous grant successes to create an ongoing and harmonious portfolio of funded projects.

INFORMATIONAL INTERVIEW

Informational interviews are an excellent way to gain valuable insights and knowledge from experienced grant professionals and grant makers. By engaging in conversations with experts in the field, you can enhance your understanding, learn best practices, and foster your continuous growth and development in the world of grant funding.

Instructions:

1. **Identify Potential Interviewees:**
   - Create a list of grant professionals, grant makers, and other individuals with relevant insights whom you would like to interview. Consider factors such as expertise, experience, and industry focus.

2. **Reach Out:**
   - Craft a polite and concise email introducing yourself and explaining your interest in an informational interview. Request a convenient time for a meeting, either in person, over the phone, or via video call.

3. **Prepare Questions:**
   - Develop a list of thoughtful questions to guide your conversation. Tailor these questions to the individual's expertise and experiences. Be sure to ask about challenges they've faced, successes they've had, and advice they can offer.

4. **Schedule the Interview:**
   - Once you receive a positive response, schedule a time for the informational interview. Be respectful of their time and come prepared with your questions.

5. **Conduct the Interview:**
   - During the interview, actively listen, take notes, and ask follow-up questions. Be respectful of their time constraints and focus on extracting valuable insights.

6. **Reflect and Analyze:**
   - After each interview, take some time to reflect on the key takeaways. Consider how the information can be applied to your own work and goals.

7. **Thank You Note:**
   - Send a thank-you email expressing your gratitude for their time and insights. Mention specific points from the interview that were particularly helpful.

INFORMATIONAL INTERVIEW

Interviewee Information:

Name:
Title:
Organization:
Contact Information:
Date of Interview:

Interview Questions:

1. What led you to pursue a career in grant writing /management/grant making?
2. Can you share a significant challenge you faced in your career and how you overcame it?
3. What are the key skills and qualities you believe are crucial for success in this field?
4. How do you stay updated on the latest trends and changes in the grant industry?
5. Can you provide insights into your most successful grant project? What made it successful?
6. What advice do you have for someone looking to advance their career in grant management/grant making?
7. Are there any common misconceptions about working in grant-related roles that you'd like to address?

Key Takeaways:

Learnings:
Actionable Steps:
Connections Made:

Next Steps:

Identify Additional Contacts:
Schedule Next Informational Interview:
Implement Insights into Your Work:

This worksheet is designed to guide you through the process of conducting informational interviews and extracting valuable information to support your continuous growth and development in the field of grant funding. Good luck!

THINGS WORTH NOTING

Why trust your memory when you can *just write it down*?

THINGS WORTH NOTING

Why trust your memory when you can *just write it down?*

Take Your Grant Game To The Next Level With These...

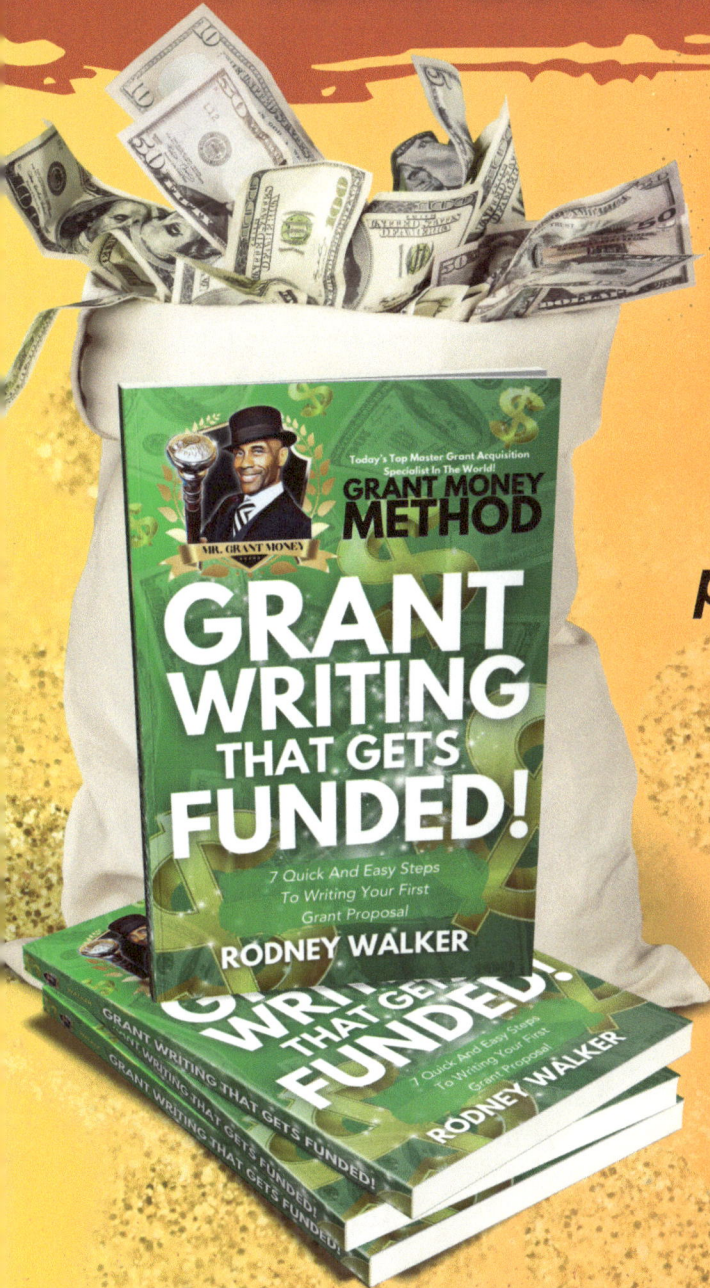

"Rodney is a grant genius! His courses are well thought out and clear, making the process of learning grant writing easier."
- Elena Esparza, Procurement/ Contract Administrator

Transform your grant proposals into lucrative successes with my proven strategies that have raised millions.

"I hit my benchmark goal of $350,000.00!"
- Rebecca Laharia

"Thank you so much for your help. Probably not a day has gone by that I didn't use something."
- Evelyn Barker, Director of Grants and Special Project at University of Texas

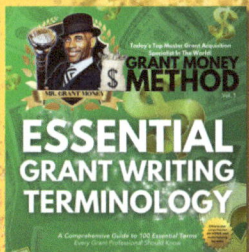

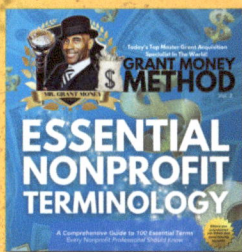

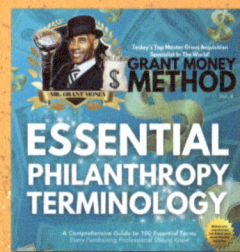

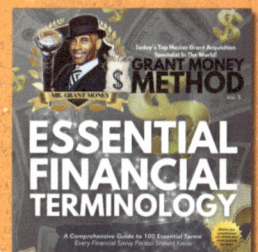

Boost your confidence in grant writing, fundraising, and finance! Elevate your communication skills with the **Fundraising Fundamentals Vocabulary Builder Series** – *100 essential terms in each series.* Invest in knowledge, empower your success!

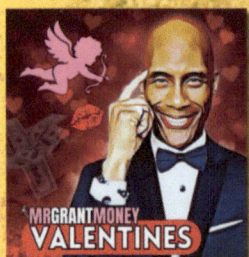

Experience Our Other Dynamic Series with Mr. Grant Money!

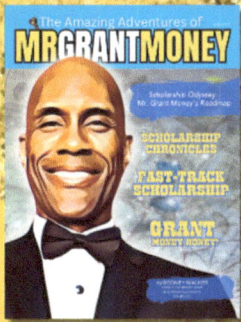

Scholarship Odyssey: Mr. Grant Money's Roadmap
Vol. 1
ISBN 979-8-89725-000-4

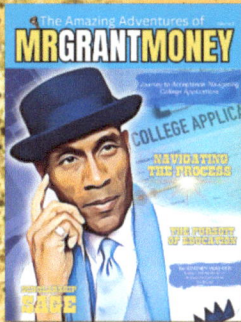

Journey To Acceptance: Navigating College Applications
Vol. 2
ISBN 979-8-89725-001-1

Passion Into Practice: Specialized Scholarship
Vol. 3
ISBN 979-8-89725-002-8

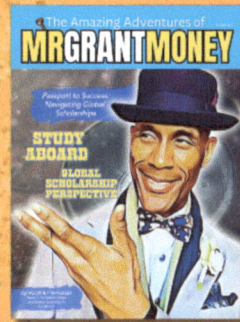

Passport To Success: Navigating Global Scholarships
Vol. 4
ISBN 979-8-89725-003-5

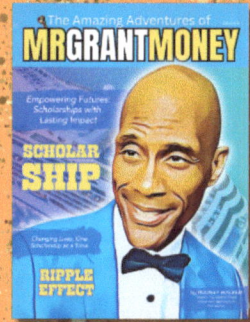

Empowering Futures: Scholarships With Lasting Impact
Vol. 5
ISBN 979-8-89725-004-2

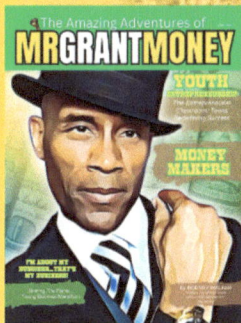

The Entrepreneurial Classroom: Teens Redefining Success
Vol. 1
ISBN 979-8-89725-005-9

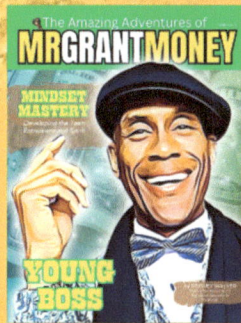

Mindset Mastery: Developing The Teen Entrepreneurial Spirit
Vol. 2
ISBN 979-8-89725-006-6

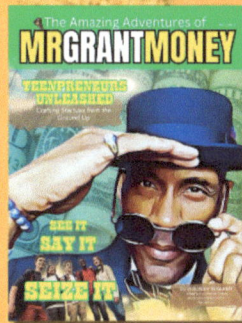

Teenpreneurs Unleashed: Crafting Startups From The Ground Up
Vol. 3
ISBN 979-8-89725-007-3

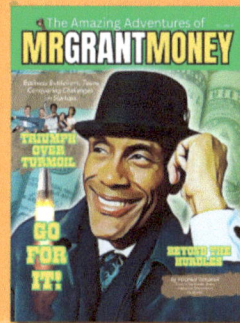

Business Battlefront: Teens Conquering Challenges In Startups
Vol. 4
ISBN 979-8-89725-008-0

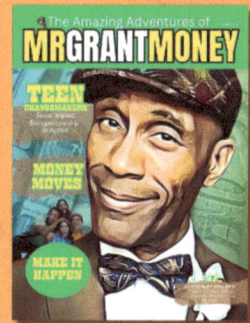

Teen Changemakers: Social Impact Entrepreneurship in Action
Vol. 5
ISBN 979-8-89725-009-7

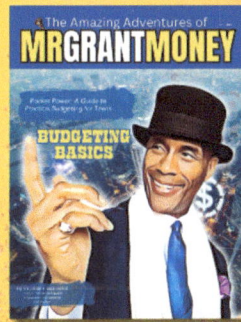

Pocket Power: A Guide to Practical Budgeting for Teens
Vol. 1
ISBN 979-8-89725-010-3

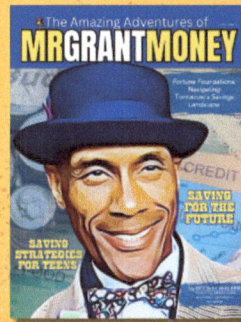

Fortune Foundations: Navigating Tomorrow's Savings Landscape
Vol. 2
ISBN 979-8-89725-011-0

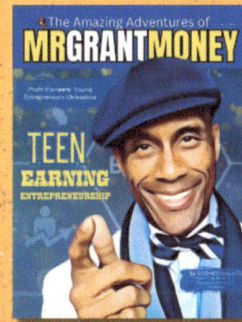

Profit Pioneers: Young Entrepreneurs Unleashed
Vol. 3
ISBN 979-8-89725-012-7

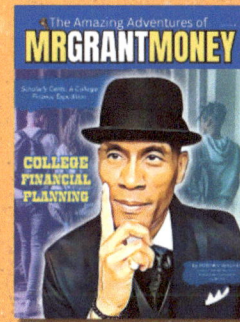

Scholarly Cents: A College Finance Expedition
Vol. 4
ISBN 979-8-89725-013-4

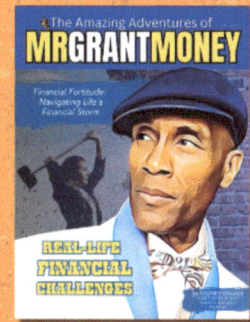

Financial Fortitude: Navigating Life's Financial Storm
Vol. 5
ISBN 979-8-89725-014-1

Enjoy More Amazing Adventures with Mr. Grant Money!

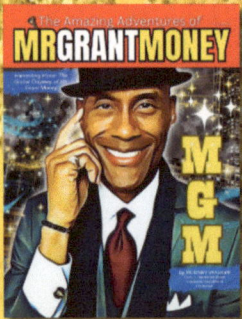

Harvesting Hope: The Global Odyssey of Mr. Grant Money

Vol. 1

ISBN 978-0-9659275-0-5

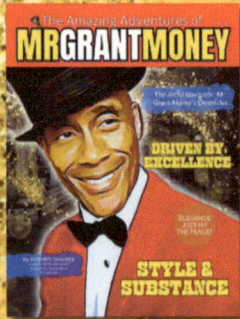

The Artful Navigator: Mr. Grant Money's Chronicles

Vol. 2

ISBN 978-0-9659275-2-9

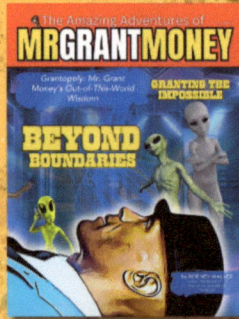

Grantopoly: Mr. Grant Money's Out-of-This-World Wisdom

Vol. 3

ISBN 978-0-9659275-3-6

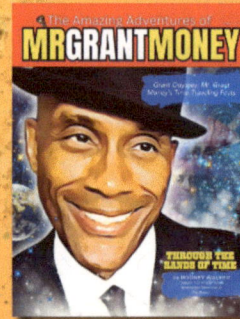

Grant Odyssey: Mr. Grant Money's Time-Traveling Feats

Vol. 4

ISBN 978-0-9659275-4-3

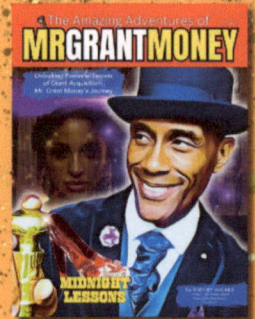

Unlocking Powerful Secrets of Grant Acquisition

Vol. 5

ISBN 978-0-9659275-5-0

Gain Exclusive Access To Companion Resources & Bonus Materials at MrGrantMoney.com and GrantCentralUsa.com

LICENSED

Bring the transformative Adventures and lessons of Mr. Grant Money to your educational institution or organization by **acquiring your license today**. Enjoy exclusive access to a wealth of online resources, such as special reports, worksheets, videos, audio training, discounts, and more, elevating the entire experience to the next level!

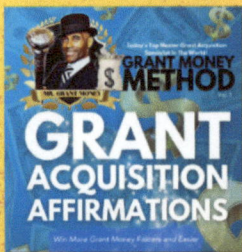

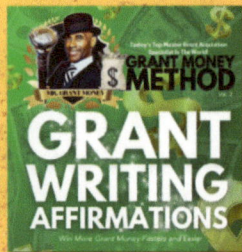

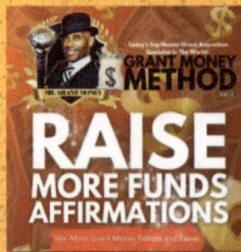

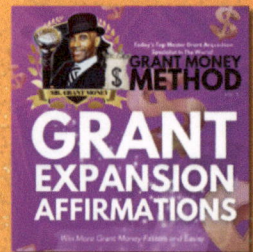

GRANT MONEY METHOD — GRANT ACQUISITION AFFIRMATIONS

GRANT MONEY METHOD — GRANT WRITING AFFIRMATIONS

GRANT MONEY METHOD — RAISE MORE FUNDS AFFIRMATIONS

GRANT MONEY METHOD — GRANT CAMPAIGN AFFIRMATIONS

GRANT MONEY METHOD — GRANT EXPANSION AFFIRMATIONS

Envision and affirm your grant success in the same proactive spirit as Mr. Grant Money. **Experience the power of these daily affirmations** to inspire and motivate your journey toward success!

www.ingramcontent.com/pod-product-compliance
Lightning Source LLC
Chambersburg PA
CBHW041450210326
41599CB00004B/195